Haunted
Minnesota

Haunted Minnesota

Ghosts and Strange Phenomena of the North Star State

Charles A. Stansfield Jr.

Illustrations by Marc Radle

STACKPOLE BOOKS

Published by
STACKPOLE BOOKS
5067 Ritter Road
Mechanicsburg, PA 17055
www.stackpolebooks.com

Printed in the United States of America

10 9 8 7 6 5 4 3 2 1

FIRST EDITION

Cover design by Tessa Sweigert

Library of Congress Cataloging-in-Publication Data

Stansfield, Charles A.
  Haunted Minnesota : ghosts and strange phenomena of the North Star State
/
Charles A. Stansfield, Jr. ; illustrations by Marc Radle. — 1st ed.
    p. cm.
  Includes bibliographical references (p.   ).
  ISBN 978-0-8117-0014-6 (pbk.)
  1. Ghosts—Minnesota. 2. Haunted places—Minnesota. I. Title.
  BF1472.U6S7264 2012
  133.109776—dc23
        2012004048

To my two fine sons—Wayne Charles and Paul Scott—
who, though skeptics on matters supernatural,
are firm believers in family, honor, and integrity

Contents

Contents

Introduction

THAT COULD NOT HAVE BEEN A FACE YOU JUST SAW, COULD IT? PERHAPS it was just a shadow, or maybe a reflection of some kind, because nobody else is in the house. Those creaking sounds on the stairs— they must be the product of an old house settling or a result of strong winds against the structure. They couldn't be footsteps, could they? There's no one there, right?

Most people have experienced puzzling sights, sounds, smells, or indescribable sensations that have no satisfying rational basis, no obvious explanation to disperse our uneasiness about them. Were they hallucinations, images originating in our brain without any external stimuli? Or was our subconscious misinterpreting real but benign and random patterns of light or sound? It has been said that humans have an inherent need to sort, categorize, and organize data into patterns and assign meaning to the meaningless.

In many cultures around the world, traditions hold that spirits of the dead are in contact with the living, and sometimes intervene in their affairs. They can perform positive roles in advising the living and protecting them from evil, as shown in the many "guardian ghost" stories. The dark side of these beliefs blames ghosts for illness, misfortune, and even death. In medieval Europe, pagan beliefs in various demons, vampires, and spectral threats were transformed by Christianity into the concept of souls trapped between this world and the next; ghosts were believed to be the spirits of those condemned by their own sins. On the other hand, many people also believe in mystical and holy apparitions, visions in which saints or angels have appeared to people in order to warn, inform, or praise them.

Religion and the supernatural appear to have a common concern in answering the profound question: is this life all there is, or are spirits eternal? Is there a way to continue after death, and can the living and the dead communicate in some fashion?

Why are certain places alleged to be persistently haunted, inhabited by ghosts that have manifested themselves to scores of people over many years? Are these ghost venues the result of concentrations of psychic energy of some form? Renowned inventor Thomas Edison conceived of our spirits as assemblages of tiny particles of energy and once declared an interest in building an electrical apparatus to facilitate communication between the living and the dead.

Belief in, or at least fascination with, ghosts, demons, angels, UFOs, and monsters is widespread. The evidence is in the tremendous popularity of these themes in contemporary culture—books, movies, television dramas, and documentaries. Stories about the supernatural are universal. Every society that exists, or has ever existed, has traditions of ghosts, demons, witches, and monsters. Public-opinion surveys assert that a minimum of ten percent, and as many as forty percent, of Americans express belief in ghosts. Clearly, if convinced believers and open-minded skeptics are grouped together, a majority of Americans are receptive to the possibility of supernatural occurrences. And even the most confident skeptics can enjoy a good story whether or not they can accept the supernatural content as real.

Ghosts are geographic in two senses. They are highly territorial. Their haunts typically are quite restricted, confined to a very specific place such as a building or a room. Ghosts can be geographic in a broader sense as well. Their personal histories and circumstances are connected to the history, geography, and culture of the environment. Many tales of the supernatural in Minnesota relate to the state's forestry, mining, and agricultural industries. Some ghosts, such as those of legendary American Indian leaders and early explorers, have historical backgrounds. Ghosts also haunt the childhood homes of a famous movie star, a Nobel Prize-winning author, and an internationally acclaimed aviation pioneer. Massive forest fires, ship sinkings, mine disasters, and mill explosions all have contributed to Minnesota's catalog of ghosts.

Introduction

You are about to begin a journey across the dark supernatural landscapes of the land of sky-blue waters. Lock the doors, turn on all the lights, sit back, and enjoy your trip. May your subsequent dreams be interesting.

The Arrowhead District

MINNESOTA'S "ARROWHEAD" GOT ITS NAME FROM ITS SHAPE ON THE map. The northeastern corner of the state tapers eastward to a point at Grand Portage. On the northern flank is the boundary with Canada, and on the southeast, the shores of Lake Superior. A line from International Falls southeast to Lake Superior just north of Duluth completes the Arrowhead.

The Arrowhead is a mostly untouched wilderness of lakes, streams, and forests, looking today much as it did when the French voyageurs first saw it nearly three centuries ago. In this beautiful region that appeals to nature-loving tourists, you'll meet Bigfoot and some exotic monsters. The phantom of a Civil War battleship haunts the lakeshore, and you'll learn how to kill a vampire, French style.

A Dark and Stormy Night

It's not easy to get lost in a town the size of Virginia, Minnesota, but the Johnsons, Larry and Janet, had managed to do just that. It didn't help that dark, thick clouds obscured the waning light of dusk. Sheets of rain swept across their windshield as they tried to read street signs. They were looking for the motel where they had reservations. Having driven up from Minneapolis, they were tired, hungry, and more than a little thirsty. A couple of cold beers would be nice, fantasized Larry. Larry was paying close attention to the road. This was Iron Range country and the area was pockmarked with open pit mines—some active, some abandoned. It wouldn't be good to miss a turn and plunge into a giant hole in the ground.

Janet was the one who first saw the girl. The car's headlights briefly illuminated the hunched figure alongside the road as they rounded a curve. There was instant agreement between the Johnsons that they should stop for the pathetic, rain-drenched figure. Normally neither would pick up a stranger, especially in a strange town. Janet's motive was humanitarian; her motherly instincts were to give the girl respite from the storm. Larry was more pragmatic. His normal aversion to asking anyone for directions had been dissolved in the downpour. Maybe the girl could tell them where the heck they were and how to find a thick steak, baked potato, and a salad bar. And some cold beer.

Larry pulled the car over on the shoulder just in front of the girl. Janet opened the door and asked the girl if she'd like a ride. The girl hesitated at first, but then nodded and climbed slowly into the backseat. The Johnsons noted that their passenger's rain-streaked face was shadowed by the hood of her thoroughly soaked sweatshirt. Long, unkempt blonde hair further obscured her face. She shivered enough to motivate Janet to turn up the heat, despite the oppressive humidity of the early-summer evening. "Can we drop you someplace?" asked Janet. "Yes, I'm going home," was the barely audible reply; "Just go four blocks straight ahead and I'll get out at the traffic light." Larry then asked, "Can you direct us to a restaurant with a bar? We need a drink and a good meal." The girl seemed to perk up a bit. "After you drop me off, turn right and then make a sharp right into the parking lot. It's a good place to eat." The girl became more animated, even enthusiastic. "Don't get the lake trout—it's frozen and has no taste. Tonight's special will be barbeque ribs. They're good. Ask for Angie, she'll take good care of you." In response to another question from Larry, the backseat guest advised him to stick to bottled beer, Canadian or German. "Jack doesn't keep the lines clean, so the on-tap beers are a little musty-tasting," she explained.

When they stopped at the traffic light, the Johnsons were surprised to see the girl run across the street and enter a cemetery. Why would she go there on such a dark and stormy night? Minutes later, they entered the recommended restaurant and asked for Angie, who turned out to be a plump, middle-aged waitress with a warm smile. Both ordered the ribs, mentioning that they'd been recommended. As they described the girl they'd given a ride, Angie's face turned white and she dropped her order pad. "Where did you take her?" Angie asked. "Well, she said she was going home, but she went into the cemetery," explained Janet. "We can't imagine why." "Because that's her home now," said Angie in a low, harsh whisper. "You gave a lift to a ghost." She went on to tell them a sad story. "Maureen— that's her name. She used to work in this place as a waitress. She was walking home one dark, stormy night just like tonight when she was struck and killed by a hit-and-run driver who was never found. There's a story going around that, on nights like this, her ghost walks around looking for her killer. I didn't believe it—until now." Larry and Janet each had a few more beers. They figured they'd need them to get any sleep that dark and stormy night.

Devil Dogs

The northern section of Minnesota's Arrowhead region is pristine wilderness. No paved roads penetrate the million-acre Boundary Waters Canoe Area, which stretches along the Canadian border opposite Ontario's Quetico Provincial Park, an equally undeveloped area. The adjacent Voyageurs National Park still looks like it did when intrepid French fur traders and adventurers first navigated the streams and lakes and marked the portages still used today. A spectacularly beautiful natural environment with few signs of humans, the northern flank of the Arrowhead seems closer to Alaska than to Wisconsin or Michigan. Bears, moose, deer, beavers, foxes, and lynx thrive here. This area also contains the last wild packs of Eastern timber wolves. The wolves are seldom seen; their intelligence and natural shyness keep them out of human sight. Likewise rarely seen, fortunately, are the fearsome, spectral Devil Dogs.

It is said the Devil prefers dogs to cats. As everyone knows, felines are highly independent creatures; even the Devil hasn't figured out how to herd cats. In Satan's opinion the unquestioning loyalty that dogs offer their masters is preferable to the calculated

self-interest of cats. That's why he enlists dogs to help in his quest for souls.

It is said that on autumn nights with a full moon, the Devil goes hunting for human souls to be dragged down to hell. The evil one becomes the great huntsman, accompanied by his Devil Dogs as aids in the hunt. The Devil rides though the night on a great black horse. Fire shoots out of the horse's flared nostrils. Black leather bags, filled with the souls of the damned, hang from the saddle horn. The pack of Devil Dogs races ahead of their satanic master, running down their targets. The coal-black dogs have red, glowing eyes. Their sharp teeth flash in the darkness as though on fire. Phosphorescent saliva drips from their open mouths. Their frenzied barking can be heard for miles, portending very bad news indeed. Those who both hear and see these spectral hounds will die that same night, or at least within the year.

Now why would the Devil choose the northern Arrowhead to ride as the great huntsman? After all, it is widely believed that Satan prefers cities to countryside, there being more unrepentant sinners per square mile in urban centers. It may be a matter of geography and nostalgia. The Arrowhead, with its glaciated, pockmarked surface filled with myriad lakes and ponds, and its dense, dark forest and relative scarcity of people, must remind Satan of Scandinavia, where he used to hunt for sport. There he was known as Odin, leader of the Wild Hunt.

Finnish Monsters in Minnesota

There seems to be little doubt that some people are much more likely to see ghosts than are other folks. These people see, or otherwise experience, ghosts in places or times that most others do not. Why that is so is a central question to many studies of the paranormal. Some students of supernatural phenomena believe that certain individuals are born with a kind of super-sensitivity to spirits. European traditions, for example, assert that people born on Good Friday or Christmas Eve have such extraordinary perception.

Some believe that the environment absorbs and retains the psychic energy of the past, in a sense recording the strong emotional traumas of past events and personalities. Can a building or part of a building be permeated by a mystical substance that records dramatic moments from the past, a "psychic ether" that preserves those images for eternity? These ghostly snapshots could then be accessed or played back as phantoms, sensed by those individuals gifted (or cursed) with extrasensory perception. Another intriguing theory is that the ability to pick up these supernatural images can be transmitted in the genes through an individual's ethnic and racial heritage. A modern Ojibwa, for example, might be especially sensitive to traditional Ojibwa ghosts and legendary monsters. Likewise, as twins Aidan and Bryce discovered, Finnish-Americans can be highly receptive to traditional Finnish spirits.

The twins were one hundred percent Finnish in ancestry, which is not all that unusual in Minnesota, where Finnish immigrants formed half the foreign-born population in the Arrowhead district during the 1890s. The twins' Uncle Otto had thrilled them with stories from Finnish folklore, stories rooted in Finland's pagan past.

Aidan and Bryce had decided to spend part of their summer vacation in the Boundary Waters Canoe Area. They had survived a challenging freshman year at the state's flagship university and were eager to get away from Minneapolis and the academic life. Canoeing into a truly wild, pristine land of forests and lakes seemed the perfect getaway. Not coincidentally, the northern wilderness of the Arrowhead closely resembled the ancestral lands of Finland that they'd heard so much about. Little did they know just how much Finnish folklore they were about to encounter firsthand.

As Uncle Otto later would explain, the twins had been extraordinarily lucky in choosing to camp under one particular enormous old pine tree. In doing so, an old Finnish custom had undoubtedly saved them from an aggressive bear. The large bear, attracted by the smell of food cooked over a fire, came right into their camp. The beast's charge was halted abruptly when it reared up on its hind legs, stared at the treetop, and reversed course. Aidan and Bryce's eyes followed the bear's line of sight toward the top of the pine tree and beheld an extraordinary sight. Impaled on a high tree branch was the sun-bleached skull of a bear. Had this odd talisman warded off an attack by the bear?

As the sky darkened at dusk, Bryce and Aidan observed orbs of light—some yellow, some blue—dancing in the darkening woods.

They were so magical and appealing that it took an effort of will not to follow them.

That night the twins had identical, very weird dreams. They saw a beautiful young girl seated by herself on a tree stump. As they watched, her face became ugly and twisted by evil. Two large rattlesnakes glided out of the woods and began to suckle at her breasts. The twins woke up in cold sweats and began preparing to head home at first light.

Uncle Otto explained it all. The twins' heritage had attuned them to traditional Finnish legends. The rugged forests and lakes, so much like Finland and permeated with the psychic footprints of early Finnish woodsmen, provided the "psychic ether" of supernatural events and creatures. The bear skull high in the tree must have been placed by Finns honoring an ancient tradition. Finns considered the bear to be a sacred animal. When one was killed, even in self-defense, a feast was held and prayers offered. The soul of the bear had to be convinced that its death was accidental. The animal's skull was placed high in a tree to help the bear's spirit go up to heaven. The skull would in turn protect Finns from bear attacks.

The bouncing balls of light were Liekko—the Finnish version of Ignis Fatuus, or "Foolish Lights" in many European traditions. The foolish thing would be to follow these glowing orbs; it is said they lead to Tuonela, the pagan Finnish land of the dead. The weird dreams showed an Ajatar, the evil female devil of the woods. She suckled serpents and her stare spread disease and pestilence. It was good that the twins did not look into her eyes.

The twins never went camping in the woods again. Folklore can be interesting, from a safe distance.

Ghost Town

Just what is a ghost town? Is it the ghost of a town, the faint apparition or pathetic relics and traces of a once-thriving community? Or is it a town now inhabited by phantoms? London, Minnesota, might qualify by both definitions.

Don't bother looking for London. It's not there anymore, at least not as a recognizable town. A careful survey of its site might uncover some crumbling building foundations hidden in the woods, but that's about it. London is, or rather was, along an old back road leading from the village of Finland back towards Route 61 and the shore of Lake Superior, about sixty-five miles northeast of Duluth.

Ghost towns—communities that grew quickly, thrived briefly, and were abruptly abandoned—usually are associated with mining towns in the Wild West. What would a ghost town be doing in Minnesota's Arrowhead district?

If Minnesota isn't generally considered part of the classic "Wild West," it certainly once was part of the Wild North. The more famous ghost towns of such states as Arizona and Colorado were abandoned when their gold or silver ran out. Minnesota's ghost towns more likely were left to rot when the trees were used up. Running out of a metal ore is understandable, but just how does one run out of trees? The present site of the ghost town of London is hard to see because of the dense forest, after all.

The answer lies in the general lack of interest in the practice of conservation back in the nineteenth century. Few were concerned with managing forests. By simply replacing trees and slowing the rate at which mature trees are harvested, forests can be never-ending sources of timber. Unlike mineral deposits, which can be exhausted, a responsibly managed forest will go on producing trees forever.

However, in nineteenth-century America, trees were stripped off the land with ruthless disregard for the future. In a vast continent with seemingly limitless resources, harvesters believed there would always be other great forests to cut. In lumber towns like London, the philosophy was "live for today, move on tomorrow." Underlying the unrestrained partying and heavy drinking in London's many saloons was a foreboding sense of an end approaching—an end to the big trees, an end to the lumberjacks' jobs, and an end for the town. Perhaps this explains the nature of the haunting at the site.

The phantoms of London are heard more often than they are seen. The honky-tonk, ragtime piano music can be heard, faintly at first, as though coming from a far-off car. The sound gradually increases in volume, becoming a pulsating rhythm that one can actually feel. The raucous sounds of drunken laughter mingle with the clinking of glasses and bottles. There is an edge to the boisterousness, an underlying hint of impending doom.

A few claim to have seen as well as heard the ghosts of London. The spirits are a rowdy lot. The old-time loggers worked hard, played hard, and drank hard. Bar brawls were common. The relative few who claim to actually have seen the phantoms of London report brawny men tossing one another across crowded saloons filled with cheering drunks. Corseted bar girls look on, their painted faces creased in cynical smiles as they raise yet another glass to the general mayhem. Large, garish oil paintings of voluptuous women hang on the walls. Card players try to stay focused on their cards as bodies and furniture fly by.

And then, all is calm. The images fade away quickly. The sounds of inebriated good times are replaced by the nighttime stillness of the forest. The loggers, the bartenders, the "soiled doves," the piano players—all are gone. The whole town is gone. The forest has grown back, reclaiming the site of the short-lived lumber town. Only the ghosts remain, drifting among the trees.

How to Kill a Vampire

Even most of the old-timers in Embarrass have no knowledge of the vampire legends about the early days of their community. Maybe it has to do with the differences in culture that evolved over the years. Those directly affected by the vampire were of French descent, but that was two hundred years ago and earlier. By 1900, most of Embarrass's inhabitants were Finns, whose own rich heritage of traditions and folklore superseded the older French legends.

Seventeenth-century French fur traders, known as voyageurs, were the first Europeans to travel regularly through the vast wilderness of the Arrowhead district. Beaver skins, much in demand back in Europe, were the prime attraction. The voyageurs, many of them based in Montreal, came by canoe to trade with the Indians. Each of these sturdy adventurers customarily carried two eighty-pound bundles of furs on his shoulders, along with his canoe, on the many portages between streams and lakes.

As time went on, some of the voyageurs settled down, establishing permanent trading posts and starting families. One of these settlers was Louis Dumont. He decided to build his store near a particularly difficult stretch of river where travelers would seek rest; "embarrass" is French for an obstacle. The river obstacle produced tired, thirsty customers for Louis' trading post-restaurant-bar, and life was good.

Then Louis' lovely young wife, Antoinette, fell ill. Her physical decline was slow but inexorable. Day by day she grew weaker and paler. It was as though her energy and vitality were slowly but surely draining away. Soon after Antoinette was in her grave, Louis took another wife. Marie, he proudly boasted, was "as strong and healthy as a plow horse," with a voluptuous body and rosy cheeks. It wasn't long, however, before Marie began to look pale and drawn. She lost weight and became listless as though losing her interest in life. As Marie lay on her deathbed, rumors began to fly. Settlers believed Marie and Antoinette had to be the victims of a vampire. At first, Louis was the prime suspect, but he passed the test: He did not flinch when confronted with the holy crucifix. Indeed, he began wearing a large crucifix around his neck.

In French folklore about vampires, the victim becomes a vampire after death. It was decided to disinter Antoinette. As her coffin was opened, the onlookers recoiled in surprise. Antoinette looked better than she looked when she died. Her skin was a healthy pink; her lips were full and red. When her mouth was forced open, it was found to be full of fresh blood. There was no doubt that she was a vampire, and thus immortal. In the French tradition, there was only one way to kill her. Accordingly, she was tied to a stake with wood piled around her and set afire. As the flames leaped around her, Antoinette's eyes snapped open and an unearthly scream issued from her bloody mouth. When the body had been consumed, the ashes were scattered in running water to prevent them from reuniting again. As soon as Marie died, her corpse was likewise burned at the stake.

One small problem remains: The settlers never caught the original vampire who killed the women. How many other innocent victims of vampires, now immortal vampires themselves, still wander the vast wilderness of the Arrowhead? The thought could, and should, contribute to a certain unease among campers, hikers, and canoeists there.

Minnesota's Own Bigfoot

Minnesota's Arrowhead country contains a vast wilderness, a pristine forest, and a lake-filled landscape of more than three million acres containing no roads or buildings. Many of the region's five thousand lakes are connected by portages, rough trails over which canoes can be carried by the strong and adventurous. There are neither roads nor railroads. Hiking and canoeing are the only means of access. The abundant wildlife includes beavers, foxes, deer, moose, and bears. And, some say, Bigfoot.

Most of Minnesota's Bigfoot sightings and stories take place in the remote wilderness of the Arrowhead. Discoveries of footprints greatly outnumber actual sightings of the legendary creature. Indeed, it was a single footprint, of which a plaster cast was made, that introduced the concept of Bigfoot to a fascinated, if skeptical, North America in 1958. A road construction crew working in a remote part of northern California discovered and documented a huge, five-toed footprint. It most closely resembled the print of a very large, rather flatfooted man or ape. A big print created by a big foot, giving rise to the name "Bigfoot."

Anthropologists and historians had long known that many Indian tribes in the Pacific Northwest had ancient legends about huge, hairy, humanlike creatures called Sasquatch. Skeptics scoffed that Sasquatch's presence in such tribal myths proved it was just a story. But these same myths also featured bears, mountain lions, and orcas, all of which are quite real.

The discovery of the California footprint led to a rise in alleged Bigfoot reports throughout the second half of the twentieth century. Footprints and sightings were reported in every state but Hawaii, and Minnesota was no exception.

The experience of one family of tourists in the Arrowhead is typical. The Archers had rented a canoe in Ely, on Lake Shagawa. They eagerly embarked on a three-day trip that they hoped would be full of fun and adventure. An adventure they got—one that they'll never forget. Their encounter with Bigfoot still haunts their dreams.

The family, two adults and two teenagers, set up camp on an empty section of lakeshore surrounded by dense woods. After a quiet night, they set off for a day's canoeing, first hoisting their food supply up into a tree to discourage bears from visiting their camp.

Just before leaving camp, they discovered they'd overlooked one tin of processed meat. "It doesn't smell of food," said Dad. "Just put it in a zipped-up sleeping bag. The bears won't be attracted."

On their return, the Archers discovered that their camp had been thoroughly but neatly investigated. The meat can, designed to be opened by pulling a metal tab, was lying near the unzipped sleeping bag. It was empty. "Well, it wasn't a bear," reasoned the father. "It had to be a human thief. Hands, not paws, opened a zipper and opened that can. But why wouldn't a thief take something else, like flashlights, Swiss Army knives, or the radio? Why not steal my Tennessee whiskey?"

That evening the family caught a quick glimpse of the probable culprit. They were sitting around the campfire roasting marshmallows for dessert after a satisfying meal. All was quiet and peaceful. Then they heard a twig snap and turned to look in the direction of the sound. Two eyes, hovering more than six feet above the ground, glowed bright red in the reflected firelight. Whatever it was it grunted and growled menacingly. Following recommended tactics for scaring off bears, the family leapt to their feet to appear larger and made as much noise as possible. Whatever was in the woods turned away and retreated. The next morning, the family found several footprints—large, humanlike prints—where they had seen the glowing eyes. They photographed the prints with a cell phone camera but had no way to cast a mold of them. A family conference decided on discretion. Not wanting to be thought of as mentally unstable or the gullible victims of a hoax, they decided to tell no one.

Scamp Knows

Some old-timers in Tofte still recall the legend of the bewitched cat that could predict the weather. Scamp was his name. Whether the cat actually had supernatural foreknowledge of storms or not is still a matter of controversy.

Fishermen, like most sailors around the world, are a very superstitious lot, perhaps due to the ever-present and unpredictable dangers of making a living out on the water. This story comes from a time when most fishermen on Lake Superior's shores were of Norwegian ancestry, except up around Grand Portage, where most were Native Americans. The Norwegians, of course, were the descendents of the Vikings, who originated many of the traditions and superstitions of the seafarers. The long-established rite, for example, of "christening" a ship at its launch by breaking a bottle of champagne on its bow goes back to Viking days. The Vikings slid a newly built boat into the water by passing it over the bodies of slain enemies, whose blood thus lubricated the boat's keel. Viking ships "born in blood" would bring luck to those who sailed in them. Gradually wine was substituted for blood.

A number of other superstitions accompanied Europeans to American shores, including the following examples: A fisherman heading towards his boat must turn back should he meet a pregnant woman on the way. A boat should be boarded with the right foot first, and, if possible, on the boat's right (starboard) side. Neptune, the god of the waters, should be appeased by tossing a penny into the water as the vessel departs its dock. A cat onboard brings good luck, unless the cat falls overboard, which signals the worst luck. The first large fish caught should be tossed back; it will guide more fish to the fishing boat. The first small fish caught goes to the ship's cat.

Scamp was a lean and hungry stray when he first showed up at Tofte's fishing docks. He was not a typical stray, however. He was clearly of aristocratic lineage, a handsome Siamese complete with the slightly crossed blue eyes typical of that breed. He was named Scamp due to his penchant for mischievous adventures. A waterfront bar provided Scamp with a bed and food in exchange for his mouse-hunting efforts.

Scamp made a habit of boarding outbound fishing boats. With Scamp aboard, fishing was good, so captains were pleased to welcome him. Then came the day when Scamp stepped aboard one boat, jumped like he was scalded, and promptly left the vessel. No amount of coaxing would lure him back. The boat sailed, with Scamp standing on the dock, watching until it was out of sight. Within hours, an unexpected storm blew up. The boat sank but the men were saved with great difficulty. How did Scamp know that disaster loomed? Did the cat have some supernatural foresight, some power to see the future? Weeks later, Scamp did it again. He would not board a boat that, later that day, was nearly lost in a sudden squall. At least in Tofte, Scamp became accepted as the judge of whether to go out or stay in port.

The Minnesota Sails On

A small fishing party aboard a private yacht out of Two Harbors saw another ship at dusk on a cloudy, misty evening. The ship was a full-rigged sailing vessel but all of her sails were furled. No bow wave formed as the wooden hull knifed through the water, nor did the ship produce any wake behind it. Most notable was the eerie silence of the ship's passage, a fact that caused the observers to doubt the evidence of their own eyes—did they or did they not see a large, antique sailing ship flash by them out on Lake Superior?

There is no doubt as to the mystery ship's identity. The many cannon bristling from her flanks reveal her to be a warship. The name *Minnesota* is displayed proudly high on her stern. An American flag flies at her masthead. She is a phantom, for the real wooden warship *Minnesota* has not existed, at least in this world, since 1901.

The United States ship *Minnesota* played a brief, mostly passive, role in a key battle of the Civil War. Although she participated heroically in a battle of great historic significance, the *Minnesota*'s role in that confrontation is memorable chiefly because of her inability to destroy her attacker. The *Minnesota*'s plight during the Battle of Hampton Roads made the ship a symbol of the necessity of adapting to change—changes in strategy, tactics, and, above all, game-changing revolutions in technology. Given the *Minnesota*'s history, her ghostly appearances may, in fact, be a warning from the patriotic spirits that we must adapt our thinking, and develop new technologies, in coping with new weapons and extraordinary challenges.

The steam frigate *Minnesota* was launched at the Washington Navy Yard on December 1, 1855. President Franklin Pierce looked on as a bottle of Minnesota water, rather than the traditional champagne, was broken across the bow. In addition to being a fully outfitted sailing ship, the *Minnesota* also was equipped with a propeller powered by two 1,000-horsepower steam engines. Carrying forty guns, she was manned by 540 men. The act of Congress that authorized the construction of *Minnesota* also funded building the

Merrimac, a ship that would play an important role in *Minnesota*'s future and, indeed, the history of the world.

On March 8, 1862, the *Minnesota* was on blockade duty in Virginia's Hampton Roads, the entrance to the Chesapeake Bay. Suddenly, a weird-looking, ironclad ship appeared. The *Merrimac*, the former Union ship since captured by the Confederates, had been rebuilt with no masts and sloping, armored flanks and renamed C.S.S. *Virginia*. The *Virginia* sank the *Cumberland* and captured the *Congress*. The *Minnesota* fought valiantly, but her cannonballs just bounced off her ironclad opponent. The *Minnesota*, maneuvering in shallow water, ran aground. As the sun was setting, the *Virginia* broke off the attack; when it returned the next morning, expecting to finish off the *Minnesota*, a surprise awaited the Confederates. The Union ironclad *Monitor* slipped out from behind the *Minnesota* and fought *Virginia* to a draw. It was the world's first battle between ironclads. In one spring morning, all the wooden warships in the world became hopelessly outdated and obsolete.

The *Minnesota* sailed on after the battle, but as a training ship for the navy. Her second career as a floating school was appropriate. The ship itself was a lesson in the necessity of new thinking, new strategies, new weapons, and new technologies. When the *Minnesota* was forty-six years old, she was decommissioned and sold for scrap. Stripped of anything valuable, her wooden hull was burned as a form of tribute to the courageous but ultimately ineffectual warship. Her burning was an echo of the proper disposal of a torn and tattered American flag—a respectful end to a symbol of courage.

The ghost of the *Minnesota* might appear on occasion as a reminder that, in a changing world, traditional thinking must evolve to include new ideas. In the supernatural world, the *Minnesota* sails again to remind us that new threats and challenges require fresh thinking and adaptability.

The Shipwreck's Ghosts

Lake Superior really is superior—it is the largest freshwater body on earth. Minnesotans boast of its beauty, fisherman can't wait to harvest its fish, and small craft owners look forward to casting off for another glorious day out on the water. But Lake Superior has a dark side, a reputation that inspires respect, not to say dread and fear, among professional sailors. Over the years, Lake Superior's rocky shores, hidden reefs, and infamous storms are said to have claimed more than 350 ships and more than a thousand souls. Not all of those souls rest in peace, as the late Howard Taylor could testify. In a way, Howard still does communicate his horrific experience with underwater ghosts, for his living descendents continue to be haunted by his stories.

Howard was very sensitive to the presence of spirits due to a childhood incident in which he nearly drowned. His was a classic near-death experience, one that he never forgot. He was at a summer camp located on a small lake. A lifeguard's attention was distracted for a crucial, almost fatal, moment, and little Howard sank beneath the surface. When dragged ashore, he was cold and blue. His breathing was restored just in time. He told of panicking for a few seconds in the icy water before slipping into a dreamlike state, warm and relaxed. He saw his dead grandparents beckoning him to join them just before rescuing arms brought him up to the surface and back into life. Ever after, Howard believed that he had, for a few brief moments, seen and heard the spirits of the dead. He kept this fleeting experience a secret shared only with his siblings.

Howard's parents had insisted that he not only go right back in the water on the day of his near-drowning, but that he become an expert swimmer. Howard had other brief underwater glimpses of spirits but tried to convince himself that he just had an overactive imagination colored by his traumatic experience as a child. Then, with a group of friends, he dove on the wreck of the *Mataafa*. There, he had the fright of his life, a scare that led him to swear that he would henceforth limit his swimming to pools, and small ones at that.

Scuba diving to explore shipwrecks has become a popular sport on the Great Lakes. The infamous violence of storms on the lakes has produced a tragically long list of interesting wrecks to visit, some of them conveniently close to shore and in shallow water. The carcass of the *Mataafa* lies a short distance offshore from Duluth and has a particularly interesting and gruesome story that produced the ghosts Howard saw.

The 4,800-ton, 430-foot-long freighter *Mataafa* departed the port of Duluth on November 28, 1905, despite a gathering storm. It was a foolish, and fatal, decision. The ship had barely made its way into the open waters of the lake when its captain decided to turn back. Huge waves, driven by seventy-mile-an-hour winds, were smashing right over the ship's decks. The captain knew that the driving rain would effectively blind him. The many large iron ore deposits in the region would make his compass unreliable. As *Mataafa* turned about, enormous waves slammed her into one of the concrete breakwaters at the harbor entrance, and then carried the ship into the other breakwater. The ruptured hull began leaking badly enough to drown the fires in the ship's steam boilers, leaving her a powerless, drifting, sinking hulk. Nine men died on the *Mataafa* that day, including four who had lashed themselves to the ship's masts for fear of being swept overboard in the storm.

It was the ghosts of those four sailors, tied securely to a sinking ship, that horrified Howard during his dive, a century after their agonizing deaths. Howard swore he saw the ill-fated men straining against their bonds, screaming in terror as the sinking ship carried them beneath the icy waves. His companion divers saw nothing unusual; Howard saw far too much to allow him to go wreck diving ever again.

Central Minnesota

THE CENTRAL THIRD OF THE STATE IS A BAND OF TERRITORY RUNNING east-west between Wisconsin on the east and the Dakotas on the west. Important towns include St. Cloud, Brainerd, Little Falls, Fergus Falls, and Montevideo. The Cuyuna Iron Range sprawls along the boundary with northern Minnesota, and to the southeast is the Twin Cities metropolitan area.

In this region, a ghost train is a reminder of a past forest fire. You'll meet the spirits of some infamous gold diggers. The phantom of the most famous pioneer aviator of all time makes a brief appearance, as does the shade of a Nobel Prize-winning author. The ghosts of Minnesota's worst mine disaster still haunt the now-derelict mine. Ghosts that may be more than six hundred years old testify to the arrival of Viking explorers in Minnesota more than a century before Columbus set sail.

Bewitched

There were nasty rumors, ugly gossip really, about the widow Lafarge. How could her farm appear to be so prosperous when her neighbors seldom saw her lift so much as a finger? Other folks in the vicinity of Bemidji back in the 1870s had to work hard for a living, but not Madame Lafarge. Her obese body seemed always to be at rest, reclining on her front porch in pleasant weather, or dining in local restaurants. She always had the money to indulge in sumptuous meals; the latest fashions in the finest silks draped her ugly body. Her house, barns, and fences always gleamed with fresh paint. Her trap lines in the woods always produced the glossiest fur pelts. Her dairy herd produced top-quality butter, not that anyone saw her work a churn. Lafarge's kitchen garden provided a cornucopia of fresh vegetables and fruits, not that she ever shared this abundance with her neighbors. How did she do it?

When her husband had committed suicide, her neighbors had tried to overcome their inherent distaste for the bereaved widow. They brought gifts of flowers, pies, and casseroles but were firmly rebuffed in the rudest way. Rumors spread that her slothful, arrogant manner had driven her husband to kill himself. In those days, the church would not bury a suicide victim in hallowed ground, which seemed to make no impression on Mrs. Lafarge. She had her husband's corpse unceremoniously buried behind her pigpen.

It became common knowledge in the neighborhood that strange sounds and weird sights could be heard and seen late at night on the Lafarge farm. Was the woman a witch, as unlikely as that seemed to the enlightened world of the upper Midwest in the 1870s? Common sense suggested staying well clear of Lafarge land, especially at night. However, as evidence shows, common sense is dissolved readily in alcohol. Late one Saturday night, two local farmhands who had consumed way too many beers decided to take a shortcut across the Lafarge farm. What they witnessed is said to have produced instant, terrified sobriety.

Hearing a great clatter on the road behind them, the men dove into a ditch. As they watched in horrified amazement, a glossy black carriage swept past them, drawn not by horses but by half-naked men in harnesses. The driver, clad in a scarlet coat and britches, cracked a long bullwhip over his sweating, panting men. "Faster, much faster—there is work aplenty for you tonight," cried the driver. As the coach halted at the farmhouse door, a suave figure emerged—none other than the Prince of Darkness, as he liked to be called. The coachman unhitched his slaves and set them to work on a variety of chores. Madam Lafarge, magically transformed into a seductive young girl, led the devil to her bedroom, promising to fulfill all of his perverted desires in a night of debauchery.

The two farmhands, still trembling from their experience, were in the front pew at church the next morning. They confided in the priest, who explained that, in ancient European traditions, those who died without confessing their sins and without the last rites were doomed to be the devil's slaves. There was, however, a way to free their souls.

Together with twenty staunch churchgoers, the farmhands and the priest returned to the Lafarge farm late that night. Arriving before the devil's coach, the priest generously sprinkled holy water on the steps of the farmhouse. When Satan got out of his coach and set foot on those steps, he screamed in agony and dove into a well shaft, descending into hell as quickly as he could. The priest, farmhands, and their associates, all armed with sharp knives dipped in holy water, rushed upon the enslaved wretches and made small cuts on their arms, thus mixing their blood with the holy water and freeing them from their bondage to evil. The widow Lafarge, it was reported, died on the spot of a massive heart attack, clutching at her chest and screaming in agony. As the crowd watched, her obese body was consumed by flames, thus ending the witch of Bemidji and her reign of terror over the devil's slaves.

Git!

"Git! Git along now!" Often, those words are heard before anything is seen, if anything is seen at all. This is one of those hauntings in which ghostly sounds are more frequently evident than visual apparitions. And, relatively unusual in hauntings, the ghosts appear, or at least are heard, over a considerable expanse of territory, in this instance a thirty-mile stretch of Kandiyohi County west of Forest City.

The hoarse commands of "Git!" echo faintly across the prairie. There is desperation and exhaustion in the heavily accented female voice. Fear and terror resonate in that supernatural voice too, for the ghost seems to be repeating an act of superhuman courage and endurance—a valiant saga of a pioneer heroine.

According to those who've personally witnessed the supernatural tableaux, it consists of a sturdy middle-aged woman driving an ox-drawn wagon. The wagon, in bad shape, also carries two men and a boy, all covered in blood and in obvious pain. The oxen, gaunt and slow-moving, are constantly urged forward by the determined-looking woman. There is no time to lose—danger surrounds them like a dense fog. The path of the wagon sometimes follows a road, sometimes just staggers across fields, apparently following a path remembered from the distant past. The phantom wagon and oxen leave no trace behind as they traverse a wheat field—no stem is crushed, no dust raised. The bloodied men and boy lying in the bed of the wagon moan as their conveyance lurches along, joined by the faint whimpers of a baby held in the mother's arms. Many believe that these ghostly sounds and images represent a recurring paranormal vision of an actual scene from Minnesota's early history.

Lars and Guri Endreson had migrated from Norway to Minnesota just as the Civil War broke out. They settled not far from Norway Lake, in an area that already held many fellow Norwegians. It was a new and thinly settled frontier, land that until recently had belonged to the powerful and aggressive Sioux Nation. The scattered army posts that had defended the frontier had lost most of their men and resources to the urgency of defending the Union. The warlike Sioux had observed the weakness of the reduced garrisons, and in August 1862 they rose against those they viewed as invaders.

When Sioux warriors descended upon the Endresons' remote farm, Guri hid in a dugout with her baby daughter. When the tumult ended, she emerged to find her husband and older sons brutally slain. Her older daughters were missing, presumably kidnapped by the marauding Indians. Her youngest son, severely wounded, had been left for dead. Most of their livestock had been stolen, leaving only two unbroken steers. Guri somehow managed to yoke the animals to a wagon and went to get help at a neighboring farm. There, she found two severely wounded men among the dead. She loaded them into the wagon with her injured son and baby and continued on her epic journey to safety in Forest City. Guri's phantom is alleged to still guide her wagon and its moaning cargo over the prairie every summer since. Hers is one of Minnesota's greatest sagas of true determination, courage, and fortitude.

Main Street's Ghost

The professor was pleased. He'd discussed the works of Sinclair Lewis so many times in his classes on modern American literature and now here he was in Lewis's boyhood home in Sauk Centre. The house, restored to its 1890s appearance, isn't actually on Main Street—it's three blocks west of Main Street on West Sinclair Lewis Avenue—but it is on Main Street in a literary sense. The novel *Main Street*, published in 1920, earned its author the first Nobel Prize for Literature ever awarded to an American. It garnered Lewis over three million dollars, adjusted for inflation. *Main Street* also angered many residents of Sauk Centre, who, correctly, saw many obvious descriptions of their town and its citizens. These references were not flattering. It took Sauk Centre a while to come around to the view that Sinclair Lewis was one of Minnesota's more illustrious sons and that restoring his boyhood home as a museum would be a suitable memorial. Maybe it would bring in tourist dollars.

The visiting professor especially enjoyed the waxwork figure of the distinguished novelist himself, occupying an upholstered rocker in the living room. The life-size mannequin was dressed in black and white, with no touch of color or flair. The figure's face had a rather grim look to it, a somewhat sour and cynical visage. Well, that's realistic, thought the professor. Lewis never smiled for the camera, and seldom smiled at anything for that matter.

The professor turned away briefly to direct his wife's attention to the figure. When they both turned to look, the mannequin, or whatever it was, had vanished. Was it his imagination, the man wondered, that the now-empty rocking chair seemed to rock slightly? Had he dreamt the whole thing or had he seen a ghost?

The professor decided to keep this sighting to himself. He couldn't afford to be regarded as a fool, a gullible victim of a prank, or a man desperate for attention. Why, he pondered, would the ghost of Sinclair Lewis return to his boyhood home? Lewis' childhood was not very happy. He was born on February 7, 1885, the son of a physician. Sinclair was a tall, painfully thin, gawky boy with a face badly pockmarked from a severe case of acne. Young Sinclair was not well-coordinated and hated sports. It became painfully obvious that his dad was disappointed in him. Scorned by his peers and lacking parental support and understanding, Sinclair ran away from home, briefly, at age thirteen.

Lewis began writing while a student at Yale University. His first efforts were, in his words, "potboilers," stories dashed off quickly and without literary merit. His first serious effort was *Main Street*, written when he was thirty-five. His other successful novels, all featuring his jaundiced view of small-town hypocrisy and narrow-mindedness, include *Babbit* (1922), *Arrowsmith* (1925), *Elmer Gantry* (1927) and *Dodsworth* (1929).

An alcoholic, Lewis checked himself in and out of several clinics over the years. He died in Rome on January 10, 1951. His cremated ashes were buried in Sauk Centre. Has his spirit chosen to return to his boyhood home because the memories of a painful adolescence became the inspiration for his books?

The Ghost of Sam Brown Rides Again

This now seldom-seen specter is at once disturbing, pathetic, scary, and sympathetic. Both man and horse clearly are exhausted, yet the horse stumbles on, urged onward by the tall, gaunt man in the saddle. The ghostly figures are hard to see in the spring storms of rain, sleet, and snow that are the last gasps of a long and bitter winter on the plains. This particular apparition appears only during such miserable weather events along the western border of Minnesota, recalling the gallant, courageous, and wholly unnecessary ride of Sam Brown.

Sam Brown, who is memorialized in a small state park in Wheaton, often is compared to Paul Revere. Revere's 1775 ride, immortalized in the poem "Paul Revere's Ride" by Henry Wadsworth Longfellow, earned him an honored prominence in American history. Sam Brown's ride is little remembered outside the plains country of western Minnesota—except, of course, by those who've witnessed the ghosts of Sam and his valiant steed.

The best time, in fact the only time, to see the phantom of Sam Brown is during the kind of miserable weather that was the backdrop of the original ride. It was one of those days when sensible people stay indoors if they can, which may explain why so few have actually seen the ghosts. Even those who think they have glimpsed

Sam are not sure exactly what they saw through the driving rain, snow, and sleet.

Compared to Sam Brown, Paul Revere had it easy. Paul's ride, which covered roughly twelve miles, lasted three hours before Revere was captured by British patrols. Sam's ride covered 120 miles and took him two days in the saddle, and in truly foul weather as well.

Sam Brown was a celebrated scout. He was very familiar with the northern plains of the Dakota Territory and western Minnesota. It was 1866, only four years after the infamous Sioux Uprising of 1862 in which more than four hundred whites had been slaughtered in Minnesota. Understandably, settlers were very nervous about any rumors of Indian hostilities.

Sam became alarmed when, serving as acting Indian agent at Fort Wadsworth in the Dakota Territory, he heard that Indian warriors were on the move, heading for the Minnesota line. Brown feared that the Indians, who had been in an ugly mood recently, were determined to murder more whites on the isolated farmsteads then springing up in western Minnesota. He donned his buffalo-skin coat and saddled his best horse. On April 19, he set out for a scouting station in Minnesota, sixty miles away. His horse struggled through snow, ice, slush, and freezing mud, falling through softening ice on ponds and streams. Thunderstorms lashed him with sleet and covered him with a coating of ice. He stopped only to warn people of a possible bloodbath. When at last he reached the scouting station in Minnesota, he learned that the warriors he had heard were on the move had just signed a peace agreement and were not a threat.

Sam Brown mounted a fresh horse and retraced his route, this time shouting reassurances of peace to those he'd previously warned of possible danger. It is said that if you spot his ghost heading east, he is frantic, screaming, "The Indians are on the warpath!" If you see his phantom heading west, he is bone-weary, dejected, and forlornly repeating, "All is well. The danger is past."

Of course, you could avoid the trauma of seeing Sam Brown's ghost by staying indoors when it is snowing, sleeting, thundering, and hailing out. Curl up with a good book and wait for summer.

The Ghostly Train of Fire

This particular horrific vision hasn't been reported much recently, which is a real blessing to those souls who've not witnessed it. For several generations of people living near Hinckley, it was a recurring nightmare: a disaster repeated again and again in the supernatural sense, or some sort of mass hysteria triggered by the ghosts of the four hundred people whose agonizing deaths were among the worst imaginable—being burned to death.

Most popular visions of hell feature fire. Doomed souls are pictured as writhing in horror amidst a permanent, searing sea of flames. For many thousands of Minnesotans living in the vicinity of Hinckley, their portion of the North Star State became hell on earth on September 1, 1894. One of the largest forest fires ever to rage in the United States took place that day, and it produced the legendary ghost train of fire.

It had been an unusually dry summer in the Great North Woods. The conservation movement, which later would be championed by future president Teddy Roosevelt, was then a radical idea of the few. Forests were cut down ruthlessly, leaving thousands of acres of stumps, broken branches, bark, and sawdust—dry timber waiting for a spark. On that fatal September day, a tornado of flame erupted southwest of Hinckley. Before it died out, 350 square miles of land, including forests, farms, and six small towns, had been reduced to ashes. Four hundred and twenty people had died as a result.

To this day, some claim the specter of the train of fire can be seen roaring down the tracks, a supernatural commemoration of a miraculous escape from unimaginably horrific death. Some believe that the appearance of the ghost train of fire can foretell a possible forest fire.

The original train of fire saved the lives of some four hundred very desperate people, and made a hero out of the train's engineer, James Root. Root was already well known at the time, having earned fame in the Civil War as the engineer of the train that carried Gen. William Tecumseh Sherman on his historic march from Atlanta to the sea. On the day of the great fire, Root left Duluth for St. Paul right on schedule at 1:55 P.M., heading down the track under a sky already dark with smoke from yet another forest fire. While forest fires were common in that era, the scale of this one, as Root and everyone else soon learned, was truly mammoth.

As the train approached Hinckley, Root saw a crowd running in panic down the tracks towards him. He stopped the train and hundreds swarmed aboard. The heat was becoming intense. Fiery embers flew everywhere. As Root backed the train away from the center of the fire, the coal in the coal car caught fire. Glass exploded in the intense heat, and the upholstered seats in the four passenger cars caught fire, as did people's clothing and hair. His hands charred from holding open the red-hot throttle, Root backed his now-blazing train up the line five or six miles until it was on a bridge over Skunk Lake. As everyone jumped off the train into the shallow water, the entire train was engulfed in flames. Seconds after being abandoned, the train was just twisted, blackened wreckage. Glass melted in the inferno. The train's reappearing ghost has haunted the tracks ever since, although the phantom train, like deadly forest fires, doesn't roll as often as it once did.

Incidentally, the loud wailing sound that is said to accompany the ghost train on its fiery run does not come from the locomotive's whistle. It is the screams of terrified passengers as their clothing catches fire.

The Ghosts of the Gold Diggers

The stagecoach moves along at a good clip. The four horses are giving it their wholehearted effort, motivated by the whip and the hoarse shouts of the driver. The driver, in turn, is motivated by the promise of a handsome tip from his passengers if he gets them to their destination a little sooner. It's Friday afternoon, and the passengers have only about forty hours in which to ply their trade. The eager passengers are "ladies of the evening," which is to say that in the world of polite, if hypocritical, society, they were not ladies at all—they were for rent. And nowadays, they are not there in the physical sense, for they, the coach, the driver, and the horses are all ghosts—mere vaporous apparitions of the former Friday stage to Springville.

This phantom stage to Springville won't reach the town, for Springville isn't there anymore. The gold-mining camp along the Minnesota River had a short, rather frantic existence from 1894 to

1896. It never was important enough to attract a railroad, which explains the stagecoach. As for the prostitutes who packed the Friday stage and left the following Sunday on the outbound stage, their weekly travels were related to a peculiar combination of Springville's public morality and private lusts and greed. Springville's citizens were strongly opposed to prostitution. Brothels were not tolerated and no ladies of the evening were allowed to live in town. It just wasn't seemly. On the other hand, the gold miners were young, adventurous, lusty men, many of them unburdened by moral restraints. If women of negotiable affection were not to be found on weekends, then these men would go elsewhere, taking their money with them and thus saddening the hearts of the town's business proprietors. An unofficial compromise was reached. The "ladies" and their unsavory trade would not be molested by officers of the law from Friday afternoon through early Sunday morning, provided they rented rooms in the town's hotel and solicited clients in saloons, not in the streets.

And so every Friday afternoon of Springville's brief life, the stagecoach would roll into town. Its cargo was gaudily dressed, garishly made-up ladies of the evening, fresh from Minneapolis. The girls were back in town, for the weekend that is.

And so, at least according to some observers, the phantom stage races towards the ghost town of Springville, which was northeast of Delhi on the banks of the Minnesota River. If you see it, it must be Friday. The ladies of the evening, incidentally, were the only financially successful gold diggers in this story. The miners and would-be miners went home poorer than they came. The tiny amounts of gold retrieved didn't cover the costs of production, not to mention those wild weekends.

The Lone Eagle Flies Again

It was almost 5 P.M. when the family of tourists was ready to leave the Charles A. Lindbergh Historic Site in Little Falls. They had enjoyed their tour of the restored childhood home of the famous aviation pioneer and agreed to fill out a brief survey form on their experience. On the question as to how they rated the opportunity to sit in the replica of the cockpit of Lindbergh's airplane, the *Spirit of St. Louis,* they checked "not applicable." The museum guide was puzzled. "Usually," she said, "visitors, especially children, like to sit in the cockpit and listen to Lindbergh's recorded voice describing his historic solo nonstop flight." "Well, we didn't want to disturb the reenactor who was in the cockpit at the time," the father replied. "He seemed to be really enjoying his role." The guide was confused: "But we never use reenactors," she said. "Perhaps you just saw a shadow as we lowered the lights for closing time."

Had the tourists seen a ghost? If the ghost was the spirit of the "Lone Eagle" himself, then why would his phantom choose to appear at the visitor center's "Spirit of St. Louis" exhibit?

Charles "Lucky" Lindbergh was born in Detroit; he was four years old when his family moved into the modest house in Little Falls where he spent most of his boyhood. In 1927, at the age of twenty-five, he became the most famous man in the world when he flew solo, nonstop across the Atlantic from Long Island, New York, to Paris. The 3,500-mile flight took thirty-three and a half hours on May 20 and 21, 1927. His courageous feat earned him instant worldwide fame, which turned out to have a dark side. Lindbergh was stalked constantly by reporters and photographers, who publicized every detail of his private life. This publicity may have included detailed descriptions of the location and layout of his New Jersey home, contributing to the gruesome kidnapping and murder of his baby son in March 1932.

The circus-like atmosphere of the trial of the kidnapper, which Lindbergh attended and appeared in as a witness, convinced him that he must leave the country to avoid the journalists, photographers, and sensation-seekers who continued to hound him and his wife. The Lindberghs moved to England; he did not move back home until Pearl Harbor was attacked in December 1941. Lindbergh had a unique perspective on World War II: Since he was the most famous aviator in the world, the Nazis allowed him to fly the latest German planes as they worked hard to convince him of the superiority of their air force. Lindbergh became convinced of German air superiority and he reported his assessments to U.S. intelligence. This belief contributed to his strong opposition to American involvement in any European war. His participation in the "America First" antiwar movement earned him the distrust of the American government. Official Washington turned against the Medal of Honor winner, which might explain why Lindbergh's spirit doesn't haunt the original *Spirit of St. Louis* housed in Washington's Smithsonian National Air and Space Museum.

The shy, intensely private man who did not enjoy the glare of unwelcome publicity has returned to this world in spirit to the place where, in life, he had felt most secure and content. There, in the precise copy of the airplane cockpit that transported him into a new world of expanding opportunities for air travel, he can revisit his hours of stress, challenge, and ultimate triumph.

Charles Lindbergh's strong but rarely acknowledged interest in the supernatural can be traced back to his pioneering trans-Atlantic flight. He did not immediately reveal his experiences with gremlins. These vaporous goblins have been reported over many years by both civilian and military pilots. The supernatural creatures have been described as either tiny human-like spirits about one foot tall or as a cross between a jackrabbit and a small dog. They sometimes play pranks on pilots but generally are considered friendly, often providing helpful advice. Lindbergh only talked about them twenty-six years after his famous flight. In his 1953 book, *Spirit of St. Louis*, he described the gremlins' appearance after nine hours of flight. The gremlins reassured him that he would make it, advised him on navigation, and provided information of a mystical nature. Do the gremlins commune with the ghost of the Lone Eagle in the cockpit replica in Little Falls? Only the spirits know.

The Shades of the Vikings

For more than a hundred years, there have been reported sightings of Viking ghosts in west-central Minnesota. It is likely that those brave enough to risk ridicule by talking about their sightings are greatly outnumbered by those who've had similar experiences but, for one reason or another, are reluctant to go public with their story. Why invite criticism or even open mockery? Seeing ghosts is controversial enough. Seeing ghosts of Viking warriors in Minnesota is absolutely beyond any stretch of paranormal possibility. Unless, of course, one knows about the Kensington Runestone. Then it might make sense, at least in the historical context.

So many sightings over so many years have led to variations in the details. Are there ten figures or as many as thirty? Are the phantoms boldly striding along or are they fearful and stealthy? Were

they bleeding from massive wounds or unscathed? There seems to be general agreement that the apparitions are those of tall, robust men wearing chainmail vests and those peculiar horned helmets popularly associated with medieval Vikings. They carry axes and swords. One moment they are there, the next there is nothing. What would Vikings, even ghostly ones, be doing in Minnesota?

It cannot just be coincidence that these Viking ghosts, while seen over a large area of Minnesota, are most likely to appear near Kensington, a tiny community southwest of Alexandria and the present home of the controversial runestone. This stone is thirty-six inches long, fifteen inches wide, and five to six inches thick. It is inscribed with runes, an alphabet used by Scandinavian peoples some six centuries ago. Debate still rages as to whether it is a hoax or the genuine article.

The runestone was unearthed on November 8, 1898, by a Swedish-American farmer living near Kensington. One popular translation reads "Eight Swedes and twenty two Norwegians upon a journey of discovery from Vinland westward. We had a camp by two skerries [rocks] one day's journey from this stone. We were out fishing one day. When we returned home, we found ten men red with blood and dead. AVM save from evil. Have 10 men by the sea to look after our vessel 14 Days journey from this island, year 1362."

If the inscription were true, the Vikings were in Minnesota 130 years before Columbus landed in America. The fact that the farmer who found the stone was of Swedish ancestry was held up as proof that it was a fake, intended to boost Scandinavian claims that Vikings had come to America long before Columbus and deserved credit as the true discoverers. When the runestone was found, most historians dismissed the Vikings' stories about "Vinland" as myth, but, in the 1950s, archeologists found the traces of an ancient Viking settlement in Newfoundland, Canada. Vinland was real. Vikings could well have sailed to the southern shores of Hudson Bay and traveled overland to Kensington, which is close to the north-south continental divide. North of Kensington, water drains towards Hudson Bay; south of Kensington, water drains to the Gulf of Mexico.

Are the Viking ghosts that allegedly haunt west-central Minnesota the shades of an ill-fated fourteenth-century expedition? As time goes on, the debate continues as to the stone's authenticity.

The Viking ghosts certainly seem as real as ghosts can be. If you chance upon them, have no fear. They have never been known to pay any attention to the living.

The Spirit of the Agitator

St. Cloud, being a university town, has seen its share of protest marches, rallies, and demonstrations. Present at all of them so far has been a tall, slender woman who is distinguished both by her fervor and her curiously old-fashioned clothing and hairstyle. She is wearing tailored trousers, a white blouse with a high neck and full, ballooning sleeves, and high-buttoned black shoes. A wooden cross hangs around her neck on a leather thong, and her graying hair is piled on top of her head in a bun. Often, she opens her mouth as though to shout along with the crowd, but no one has ever heard her voice. Perhaps that is not surprising, for she is a ghost.

The ghostly presence can be spotted participating in acts of civil disobedience on campus. If approached too closely by the living, she quickly fades away, dissolving in a small cloud of smoke. Those who combine a belief in ghosts with knowledge of St. Cloud's history believe that this phantom supporter of civil rights is the spirit of Jane Swisshelm.

When Jane Swisshelm arrived in St. Cloud in 1857, she already had earned a reputation as a noted author and lecturer and a fearless campaigner for personal freedoms and rights. Born in western Pennsylvania to serious-minded Scots-Irish immigrants, she had a stern, no-nonsense view of life and a passionate hatred of slavery. While living in Kentucky, she observed slavery firsthand and began writing articles denouncing the "evil institution," as she called it. Jane became active in the Underground Railroad aiding runaway slaves.

Jane's husband, James Swisshelm, was a failure as a businessman. In one peculiar episode, James traded a failing business enterprise for a live panther and two bears, evidently with thoughts of setting up a circus. To his surprise Jane objected to having a panther and two bears in the household. Jane left, taking her infant daughter with her, and went west in search of a new life. In St. Cloud, she got herself a job as editor of the *Minnesota Advertiser*, which she soon bought and renamed *The Visiter*.

Jane had a lot of strong opinions, which she advanced in equally strong language. She seems not to have heard of, or she just didn't care about, laws concerning libel. *The Visiter* contained vitriolic attacks on slavery, slaveholders, and friends of slaveholders. Jane enjoyed demolishing the reputations of those who opposed her. She took on a local landowner and influential entrepreneur, Gen. Sylvanus "Sam" Lowry. Sam was a Southerner who routinely brought household slaves to St. Cloud from his plantation, even though Minnesota was a free state. This incensed Jane, who relentlessly attacked Lowry in print, along with his family and associates.

Jane smeared enough important people to invite scores of lawsuits against her. At a meeting with General Lowry, she agreed to cease attacking him and his friends in *The Visiter*. She then changed the name of her paper and resumed her inflammatory editorials in the new paper, thus keeping her promise about *The Visiter*. When the Civil War broke out, Jane volunteered as an army nurse.

Jane eventually retired to a small cabin in western Pennsylvania where she continued to write in support of civil rights and personal freedoms. Her spirit still marches on, quite literally. In life, Jane Swisshelm spoke her own mind with reckless determination. Many believe that her crusading spirit is still at the forefront of the causes of liberty and equality.

The Wailing Siren

The Milford Mine near Crosby is haunted, and for good reason. Forty-one miners died there on February 5, 1924. The following day, the widow of one of the victims of the disaster committed suicide in the mine, joining her husband in death. The Milford miners drowned in an underground flood, a particularly agonizing and prolonged death. They had to have known that the swiftly rising waters were about to snuff out their lives and that their futures were measured in minutes and seconds.

The miners had accidentally cut into an underground aquifer, a water-transporting rock strata that was, in effect, an underground river. As the dark tunnels began to flood, the miners desperately sought higher shafts and branch tunnels. Near-freezing water steadily crept ever higher on their bodies. Their screams were echoed at higher volume by the ear-piercing shrieks of the emergency sirens. They were trapped. It is said that the sounds of the pitiful moans and agonized cries of the miners and the unrelenting wail of the siren were heard throughout the mine even after it was pumped dry and reopened. Allegedly, many men entered the reopened mine to work, only to leave abruptly before their shift was over, badly frightened by the spectral sounds and the sight of the disaster victims.

Miners tend to be superstitious, a product, perhaps, of their extremely hazardous work environment. It has to be unnerving to realize that thousands of tons of rock and soil lie over one's head. Tunnel collapses are not uncommon. Falling rock can kill instantaneously or, by blocking off air, slowly suffocate the unlucky. Poisonous gases can accumulate underground; if undetected, they can kill stealthily and silently. Or, as in the Milford Mine, a sudden inrush of water can overwhelm the strongest men in a few minutes of terror. Many miners leave the mines seemingly unscathed but with lungs clogged with rock dust that will slowly suffocate them, draining their energy and dooming them to years of gasping and struggling for every breath.

There are many ways to die in mines, and most miners believe strongly in luck, both good and bad. Mine rats, for example, can bring good luck. They are thought to be especially attuned to any vibrations in the rock that could presage a tunnel collapse. If the rats suddenly decide to head for the surface, prudent miners should do likewise. Accordingly, mine rats are to be befriended by leaving out food scraps for them. Killing a mine rat would be akin to killing a dog above ground. The mines are also thought to be inhabited by mischievous spirits, or tommyknockers. Tommyknockers are not really evil but can be annoying. They can hide tools, cause lights to go out, and trip men.

It is reported that many of the bodies from the Milford disaster were not found until months after the mine flooded. The final corpse was located a full year after the disaster. A common theme in ghost lore is that the spirits of the dead are condemned to wander until they are reunited with the body as it is buried with proper dignity and appropriate ritual. Sudden, violent, or especially agonizing deaths also are known to produce ghosts. The Milford Mine was so haunted by the specters of the dead miners that other miners eventually refused to work there and it had to be abandoned.

The miners who had, briefly, worked in the reopened mine claimed that the intense horror of the ghosts' cries and moans so filled their minds that they could not concentrate on their work. Especially unnerving was the eerily wailing siren sound.

The supernatural siren is associated with the most famous ghost in the Milford Mine. Harley Harris was in the mine when the waters invaded. He sounded the emergency siren and stayed at his post, keeping the siren operating to warn others to leave if possible. As the rising waters diminished his chances of escaping, Harley tied himself to the siren so that, even in death, the weight of his body would keep the siren operating.

In Crosby, there are those who believe they can hear the siren during the still of the night. The Milford Mine long has been closed to the living, but the ghosts are there yet.

Two Aces Beat Two Kings

In the venerable game of poker, two aces always beat two kings. But when two aces beat two kings seven times in succession, a man has to wonder whether he's playing with honest men. Poker players know the odds, and the odds just don't favor those kinds of hands seven times in a row. A thoughtful man might well conclude that someone is cheating and demand his money back, at the point of a gun if necessary. Such incidents were famously numerous in the mining and cattle towns of the Wild West. But in staid, small-town Minnesota? Oh, yes. A sharp disagreement about the integrity of a group of card players led to murder in Little Granite Falls on April 1, 1901. A ghostly quartet followed the murder.

According to legends, some apparitions are quite predictable and consistent, appearing on schedule as though punching a time clock. Not so with the poker game phantoms. Their manifestations are on some devilish timetable of their own devising. The only common thread in their erratic appearances is that they apparently prefer late-night hours in dental or medical offices. Perhaps the choice of time and location explains the rarity of reports of these particular ghosts.

As recounted by observers, the ghosts of four men are seated around a table. Three are models of sober, middle-class respectability, wearing neat but unremarkable clothes. The fourth gentleman is flamboyant in appearance, clad in a tan and green-checked tweed suit and a bright green embroidered vest with a purple silk tie. He has a diamond tiepin and several gold rings. In life, his name was William Lenard but he liked to be known as the "Irish Lord," telling folks that he was the son of aristocrats. Lenard had been a well-known, if rather shady, character in St. Paul, where he amassed more than fifteen thousand dollars in poker winnings. Suspicions of cheating led Lenard to conclude that leaving town would contribute to a longer lifespan.

In frequent visits to Granite Falls' more elegant saloons, William let it be known that he was interested in playing high-stakes gentlemen's games if anyone was sufficiently sophisticated and adventurous to accommodate him. Several local dudes rose to the bait. Such games were best kept quiet and private, so it was agreed that the game would be held in the offices of Dr. Samuel Wintner, a prominent dentist. Conveniently, the offices were located over a liquor store, allowing refreshments to be quickly assembled.

The game had gone on for twelve hours when Dr. Wintner observed, through a haze of smoke and whiskey fumes, that his encouraging possession of a pair of kings was beaten by the Irish Lord's pair of aces—seven times in a row. The angry doctor forcibly pointed out the extreme unlikelihood of this unbroken string of such defeats. The Irish Lord just laughed. The dentist demanded the prompt return of the two hundred dollars he had lost. Lenard refused and called Wintner a sore loser, a Welsher, and a crackpot and suggested that the dentist's father had not bothered to marry his mother. Wintner excused himself, left the room, and returned with a pistol, which he held to Lenard's head. The Irish Lord called the doctor's bluff with a drunken smirk. Big mistake. After shooting the cheater, Dr. Wintner knocked out the man's teeth with the butt of the gun.

During the murder investigation, police found many marked decks of cards in Lenard's rooms. Many St. Paul citizens testified that the Irish Lord was a phony and a cheat. At trial, the defense argued that Dr. Wintner was trying to prevent further felonious actions by the despicable cheat. The jury agreed. Dr. Wintner went free to return to his drill and pliers. Two aces still beat two kings, but a gun beats a marked deck.

Northern Minnesota

THIS LARGE REGION STRETCHES FROM THE CANADIAN BORDER SOUTH-ward to a line between Duluth on Lake Superior and Moorhead on the North Dakota border. Important towns include Bemidji, Crookston, Hibbing, and Grand Rapids. Much of Minnesota's iron ore comes from the Mesabi Range, which is shared with the neighboring Arrowhead district.

Northern Minnesota's tales of the supernatural feature the state's first peoples and their cultural traditions, such as the mysterious Windego. You'll meet the spirit of one of Hollywood's greatest stars at her childhood home. A possible early version of the Bigfoot legend occurred here.

Faces in the Flames

Eric had been fascinated by flames for as long as he could remember. The dancing, writhing brightness had a mesmerizing effect on him; he found it both fascinating and soothing. If he was a little sleepy, a fire's ever-shifting kaleidoscope of shapes in every possible shade of red, orange, and yellow would ease him into "dreamland" as his mother put it. The flames were so reassuring, so restful in the way they endlessly repeated the familiar combinations of shapes and colors but with continual variations. Eric always was sad to see the end of the flames, when the vibrant, throbbing color was replaced by black—the complete absence of color.

Eric's intensely focused interest in watching the flames caused some anxiety in his parents. At his childhood birthday parties, he would refuse to blow out the candles on his cake. His parents worried they were raising a firebug. Actually, it was quite the opposite. Eric liked to watch flames that were safely contained, restrained in the glass shield of a lantern or imprisoned behind a metal fireplace screen. To Eric, fire was a living thing, a symbol of life. To him, the common phrase, "the flames died" was quite literally true. Flames were alive, but they had the power and potential to destroy and kill in a most agonizing and merciless way. Eric knew this because the faces in the flames told him so. And they told him over and over again, relentlessly and emphatically.

Eric always had seen faces in the flames. Childlike, he had assumed that everyone saw them. Sometimes the faces, which appeared only for the briefest of moments, were readily recognizable, sometimes not. The appearance and disappearance of the faces took place as swiftly as the fleeting image of one or two frames of a motion picture—time enough only for a quick flash to the brain of a picture, with no second chance to look for more detail or to confirm an initial impression. To his growing amazement, and not a little horror, Eric came to realize that the faces he glimpsed before they twisted away in the wavering flames were those of people who had very short life expectancies. What he was seeing in the flames was the approach of the angel of death. Why was he blessed—or cursed—with this most disturbing foreknowledge?

His familiarity with family history, supplemented by the tragic story of the destruction of his hometown of Cloquet, provided the answer. Eric had somehow inherited the ability to sense the approach of death from an ancestor who had had the searing experience of watching death come for him in the form of fire. Death by burning, so horrifyingly painful that it once had been inflicted on witches, was so traumatic that its victims' spirits could never rest in their graves. In legend, the souls of those who died by fire were doomed to wander the earth, repeatedly invading the subconscious of their living descendents to warn that death was near.

As Eric was well aware, one of his ancestors had died in the Great Fire of October 12, 1918. This destructive fire literally raced across the area, driven by seventy-mile-an-hour winds. Two thousand square miles were reduced to ashes, four hundred people died, and more than two thousand people received disfiguring burns. Cloquet was almost totally destroyed. When rebuilding, Cloquet's residents strongly preferred brick over wood, though the timber industry remained the town's chief source of employment.

Nearly a century after that catastrophe, Eric, and doubtless others, are haunted by the sad burden of foreknowledge of impending death. Still, Eric cannot avoid staring into the flames of prophecy, knowing that some day he will see his own face portrayed there.

Going Back in Time

Jim Cross was very careful about who he told about his supernatural trip back in time. He was a salesman, a very good salesman in fact, and couldn't afford to be thought of as weird. For years after the event, he told no one. After Jim retired and concluded that he no longer had to worry if customers might think he was delusional or simply lying, he told a few friends, swearing them to secrecy.

The incident in question had happened after Jim had enjoyed a profitable morning calling on old customers in International Falls. Despite a forecast of snow, he decided to drive on to Bemidji after lunch. After all, if you are living in Minnesota, you can't avoid driving in snow, unless you can hibernate longer than bears. He followed the highway west of International Falls, paralleling the Rainy River. He didn't get very far. Heavy snow, accumulating fast, was driven into high drifts by a fierce northwest wind, and night was fast approaching. Even Minnesotans have to know when to stop ignoring Mother Nature and seek shelter. He spotted an "Open" sign on a bed-and-breakfast inn, an unexpected and most welcome sight.

The middle-aged proprietress was happy to welcome him. "You have your choice of rooms," she said. "You're the only guest." Upon inquiring about dinner, Jim was told that the innkeeper stocked only breakfast foods, but she could supply pancakes, bacon, and eggs. "Fine," he replied, and he enjoyed the meal. He retired to his large, comfortable room in the impressive Victorian mansion. It had been a long day, and he was soon asleep.

Jim awakened to the sounds of merriment. Against a background of lively music he could hear the kind of loud laughter and conversation that, in his experience, characterized a party where most guests were well beyond the second drink. He just could not get back to sleep. Glancing out the window, he saw that the parking lot was filled with magnificent old cars, all of 1920s vintage. Jim was a fan of antique automobiles and he saw below him an assemblage worthy of a museum. Gleaming Chryslers and Cadillacs, Packards and Pierce Arrows, even a stately Rolls Royce were parked next to Jim's humble-looking Honda. His curiosity aroused, Jim got dressed and went downstairs. He was welcomed to the party with drunken enthusiasm. The gentlemen wore tuxedos while their ladies showed off the latest fashions, at least for 1925: short, shimmering dresses covered in glittering beads. The ample bar displayed the most prestigious brands of Scotch and Irish whiskey, English gin, Polish vodka, and French champagne. Jim happily joined the party.

When Jim awakened, it was almost noon. To his relief, he did not have a hangover, though he could remember having had quite a few drinks. He dressed and packed and went down to breakfast. "Sorry to be so late," he said. "No problem," replied his hostess. "You won't be able to leave until they plow the roads." Jim looked out at the snowy parking lot, occupied only by his Honda, covered in at least a foot of snow. "Where did all the old cars go?" he asked. "What cars?" she replied. "You can see by the deep snow that no one has come or gone since you arrived." "What about the party last night?" he queried. "There wasn't any party last night," replied the hostess. "How could there have been in the middle of a blizzard?" Over his second cup of coffee, Jim inquired into the history of the place. "Well," she said, "My great-grandparents used to operate a famous—or infamous—roadhouse here back in Prohibition. It was easy to smuggle in illegal booze from Canada, just a short distance across the Rainy River. In winter they could drive across the frozen river and in summer they could use small boats. People would come all the way from the Twin Cities to attend parties here. Even including some gangsters, or so they say."

To this day, Jim Cross is convinced that he had somehow travelled back in time that night. Or was it all a dream?

Judy's Ghost

Unlike her big sister Gloria, Marie was not very interested in the supernatural—until, that is, she began seeing a ghost. The ghost wasn't your typical phantom of a deceased loved one, either. Marie believes that she has seen, on multiple occasions, the spirit of Judy Garland.

Among ghosts who have been seen, heard, or otherwise sensed by many people over a lengthy stretch of time, most had some claim to fame, or notoriety, in life. Presidents, military leaders, movie stars, and infamous criminals all seem to reappear after death with greater frequency than unknowns. These supernatural returns to the public eye might be attributable to the powerful personas that made these people famous, or the strong desire of many of their admirers and fans to believe that they've glimpsed the shades of legends. Many really want to believe that these famous persons of the past are still participating in the nation's culture, even if only as spirits.

Marie had no expectations of meeting Judy Garland's ghost when she took a job at the Judy Garland Museum in Grand Rapids. Marie was a fan of the acclaimed actress and singer but she wasn't compulsive about her admiration, and certainly wasn't fixated on encountering Judy's spirit. It took Marie some time to realize that she had seen Judy's ghost, because the phantom did not take the familiar form of the teenager who rocketed to stardom in the 1939 classic *The Wizard of Oz*. Nor was the ghost in the likeness of the mature woman.

Garland's ghost assumed the image of a little girl of about four years. The tiny figure (as an adult, Judy stood only four foot eleven) appeared in the garden by her childhood home. The phantom, as described by Marie, is the picture of carefree, innocent joy in life. The ghost perfectly captures the radiant happiness of a bright and beautiful child, full of anticipation of all of life's wonders before her. There is no mystery as to why Judy's spirit would materialize as a four- or five-year-old, for she is celebrating a truly happy phase of her life, a life that was later burdened by many tribulations in her teenage and adult years.

Judy, born Frances Ethel Gumm in 1922, began appearing onstage as a toddler. She signed a movie contract with MGM when she was only thirteen. She grew up on movie sets, where she couldn't relax between takes like the other actors—she had to do her schoolwork under the direction of a tutor. She appeared in thirty-three feature films. The incessant pressure doubtless contributed to her tragic dependence on drugs. Despite her struggles with drugs, alcohol, wildly fluctuating weight, and the disappointments of five marriages, Judy reshaped her show-business career to become a highly successful singer, with sold-out stage performances and many televised specials. She died in London at the age of forty-seven, the victim of an apparent overdose of prescription medication.

Her carefree childhood days were painfully short. No wonder that the great star's spirit chooses to revisit her pre-Hollywood days in Grand Rapids, a time of innocent joy at life's prospects. Wish her spirit well if you sense her supernatural presence—her life was less kind after she left Minnesota. Her "yellow-brick road" led to an adulthood of many challenges.

Shades of the Cow War

The border was tense. The defenders, members of the Minnesota National Guard, were nervous. Their mission was to defend the border and repel invaders, but how much force was authorized? Was deadly force permissible? Would the border incursions escalate to all-out war? Would the soldiers ever again see their homes and loved ones?

It took some getting used to, this thinking of the outsiders as the enemy, though of course they were. It was a matter of survival, of protecting their homeland, of preserving their economic lifeblood. The invading hoards were voracious, capable of destroying the basic resources of the land they were invading. They appeared to have no scruples about doing so, their desperation was so great. And yet, the invaders' plight was understandable to the guardsmen; to a degree, the defenders were sympathetic. The ultimate cause of the crisis was beyond any man's, or any government's, control.

The phantoms are reenacting the Cow War, an infamous 1934 episode in which Minnesota's northwestern border with North Dakota became contentious. No one was killed in the Cow War, so what motivates the ghosts to reappear along the Red River every summer? What powerful trauma in their lives would explain the spirits' compulsive return?

The traumatic event that led to the Cow War was the great "Dust Bowl" of the 1930s on the Great Plains. As people learned the hard way, rainfall on the plains, the "tan midriff" of the continent, was extremely unpredictable. Long-term averages of precipitation just didn't tell the story. Very dry years and comparatively wet years could occur without warning. There seemed to be a series of cycles of unusually dry or wet years, but these cycles were of unpredictable length, and could be interrupted by a wet year in a dry cycle or a dry year in a wet series. It was enough to drive a man to drink, if he could find water, that is, as an old joke went. It certainly drove men to take desperate measures, including the decisions that led to the Cow War.

In the severe drought year of 1934, the northwestern part of Minnesota was not hit as hard by drought as was neighboring North Dakota. North Dakota's ranchers watched helplessly as their cattle starved on the shriveled, dead grasses of the bone-dry plains. Across the Red River to the east, Minnesota's grasslands seemed in better shape. Many North Dakota ranchers decided to move their cattle to Minnesota, without, of course, consulting Minnesota landowners. This "invasion" would be but a short-term gain for the invaders; in the long run, running more cattle on the same land would inevitably lead to a deterioration of the environment. Too many hungry cows on too little grass would literally eat up the resource and everyone would suffer. Without grass roots to hold topsoil in place, the precious resource would blow away. Minnesota governor Floyd Olson issued a decree that no cattle should cross state borders and ordered the state's National Guard to the border to enforce the edict.

More than seventy years after the standoff, a group of students from the state university branch at Crookston had an interesting encounter with the shades of the Cow War. They were on a summer camping trip and set up camp on the banks of the Red Lake River, not far from the Red River border with North Dakota.

Now, truth be told, their collective experience with the supernatural was preceded by the consumption of a case of cold beer. The students, however, swear that their fright produced instant sobriety. At dawn's first light, they were awakened by the thunderous sound of a large herd of cattle rapidly approaching from the west. The frantic animals were heading directly for their campsite. A horrific, painful death by trampling under hundreds of sharp hooves seemed to be the students' certain fate. Then, miraculously, a ragtag line of uniformed guardsmen appeared, firing their rifles in the air. Abruptly, the charging cattle simply evaporated, as did the defending guardsmen. All that was left was a haze of fine dust in the air and some badly shaken students. Did it happen or did all the students have an identical nightmare? They still are not sure, but they don't do much camping near the border anymore.

The Earliest Bigfoot Sighting

The long-abandoned town of Bloomer, no longer on the map, was northwest of Warren, up near the northwest corner of the state. Bloomer's transient existence must have been based on serving as a trade center for local farmers; its sole mention in Minnesota's history is as the locale for the discovery of a briefly famous fraud. This particular fraud, however, was inspired by a confrontation with Bigfoot that may or may not have been a fraud, depending on who you believe.

The verifiable facts are few. A road crew was digging a culvert on a road in Bloomer on June 8, 1896. To their great amazement the crew uncovered what seemed to be, at first, a beautifully detailed statue of a very muscular man. Some of those present, however, doubted that the object was a statue. Who could have created such a wonderful work of art out on the recently settled prairie? The face was neither that of an Indian nor a European. The figure was five feet nine, with disproportionally long arms and large feet. The jaw thrust forward and the brow was very prominent, giving the face an apelike appearance.

Local "experts" declared that it was not a statue but a petrified man. The *Minneapolis Journal* reported the discovery: "Nature has in a wonderful manner preserved the form and features of this man in a far more perfect condition than in any Egyptian mummy embalmed by the hands of man . . . certain it is from many proofs that the body has been in the ground at least 150 to 200 years, and possibly for a far longer period." The tenant of the farm where the "petrified man" was found sold the figure for $175 to someone who put it on display in Crookston and charged admission to view it. The relic was then sold to a traveling carnival for $1,000. Shortly afterwards, the molds in which the petrified man had been manu-factured were found in a plasterer's shop in Crookston.

At the time, it was assumed that the clever plasterer had tried to cash in on the long-running American fascination with alleged pet-rified prehistoric men. Invariably, these relics became the featured attraction in traveling shows and earned a lot of money. The first such fake was the "Cardiff Giant," a ten-foot tall "primitive man" unearthed in Cardiff, New York, in 1869. The Cardiff Man was so popular that legendary showman Phineas T. Barnum tried to buy it. When he was turned down, Barnum had a replica made. Other fake petrified giants were "found" in New York, Colorado, and Montana before the Bloomer "discovery."

The Crookston plasterer who admittedly created the petrified man, however, made no attempt to claim ownership or capitalize on his artwork in any way. Why not? And why make his figure of only average height when all the other frauds were giants, inspired by the Biblical report in the Book of Genesis of "giants in the earth"? Something did not fit.

A descendent of that plasterer who wishes to remain anony-mous told the real story of the "Bloomer Man." According to family tradition, the figure was an accurate model of an apelike creature whose dead body had been observed by the plasterer when he was out duck hunting by himself at dawn. The story was that he stum-bled across the fresh corpse and was examining it when two much larger creatures showed up and frightened him away. The two new-comers were eight to nine feet tall. They carried away the smaller body, evidently that of an immature male. From the description confided in his family, the plasterer had seen what we would call Bigfoot, or rather two adults and one juvenile of that species.

The plasterer was understandably concerned that reporting his observations would land him in an insane asylum or at least make him the object of scorn and derision. He decided instead to make a replica of the body he had examined so carefully and plant it where he knew it would be found. He was curious to know what anthro-pologists would make of it. He was as surprised as anyone when "experts" declared it to be a petrified primitive man and turned it into a sideshow freak. If only everyone knew the real story!

The Ghosts of Hibbing

In the lore of ghosts, goblins, and hauntings, it is a well-established principle that the dead do not like to be disturbed during their big sleep. Disturbing the deceased by literally uprooting them is tantamount to soliciting supernatural vengeance. The moral of countless ghost stories is that the dead should be left in peace lest they destroy the peace of the living.

Another common theme in ghost stories is that death seldom alters substantially the personality of the once-living person. The spirit often portrays the living soul's positives and negatives in exaggerated fashion but rarely reverses them. A devoted caregiver in life, for example, likely will become a so-called "guardian ghost," a spirit still seeking to protect and comfort the living. On the other hand, a foul-mouthed brawler's ghost will continue to behave, or misbehave, as the supernatural clone of the deceased troublemaker. The ghosts of some of Hibbing's earliest citizens make for some scary apparitions, given their life histories and the circumstances of their disrespectful and calamitous disinterment and reburial. These ghosts are grisly visions of outrage and determined vengeance.

Now the largest of the Iron Range towns, Hibbing was born as a lumbering center. In 1893, a portable sawmill was hauled through the forest and set up at Hibbing. A rough-and-tumble community grew up quickly, one that would make the notorious mining towns of the West look like sedate monasteries. The lumberjacks were an infamously hardworking, hard-playing, and hard-drinking lot. Theirs was an especially dangerous and physically demanding job, one that encouraged a fatalistic view of life and death. Large, prosperous saloons featured "snake rooms" where drunks could lie on the floor in a stupor until they had "slept it off." Foremen from the lumber company would round up the men in the morning and transport the groggy workers into the forest or to the mills.

The town really became rough when it was discovered that Hibbing and the vicinity lay atop a huge deposit of high-quality iron ore. The recent immigrants who formed the mining workforce made the lumberjacks look like Sunday school teachers. Political corruption took place on a grand scale, matching the ruthless exploitation techniques of the big lumber and mining companies. One election saw a winning margin of 1,100 votes—even though registered voters numbered about three hundred. In another dubious election result, the citizens "voted" to sell the entire town, and by extension the valuable ore underneath it, to a mining company.

In 1921, the entire town—stores and houses, saloons and churches—was put atop log rollers and dragged a mile or two to the south. The dead were not left behind in the move. In the words of a contemporary observer, graves were "reverently scooped up with steam shovels" and the occupants given new resting places. Except that the dead did not rest.

The jagged-edged steel buckets of the steam shovels, however "reverently" directed, tore open multiple graves at a time, pulverizing coffins and smashing corpses. Splintered bones and crushed skulls were intermingled in a horrific jumble. The replacement coffins were filled with an assortment of bones with no way to determine which fragment had belonged to who.

The spirits of those whose mortal remains were treated so disdainfully are, to put it mildly, enraged. Some claim that the angry ghosts of Hibbing's early days can be seen hovering over what is now an open-pit iron mine. These phantoms appear to move about on a surface that no longer exists—the former ground level that existed before the town was relocated. Greed motivated the removal of their graves; callous indifference mangled their corpses and mingled their remains. Beware the disturbed—and disturbing—ghosts of Hibbing.

The Legend of the Windego

Many cultures around the world have traditions of death omens. In many folk beliefs, the harbinger of death is a black creature—a bat, a crow, a raven, or a cat—that hangs about the home of the person who will soon die, behaving in an uncharacteristically erratic and hostile manner. In the ancient traditions of several North American tribes, including the Objibwa people of northern and western Minnesota, the Windego was a death omen.

The Objibwa's Windego, in contrast to the other omens, is dazzlingly white in appearance. While humanlike in form, it is described as fifteen feet tall. It wears a pure-white garment that is

gauzy or lacy in texture, flowing loosely around its body. The Windego's face has a fierce expression, with a death head's grimace of sharp and stained teeth and red, glowing eyes. There is a star imprinted on its forehead. The Windego can appear at any time of day or night. Its pace corresponds with the timing of the approaching death. If the Windego is running, death will strike soon, perhaps within hours. If the Windego walks slowly, the impending death may occur in a few days. Should the Windego stumble, there is the possibility that death might be averted by observing cleansing rituals for all of one's family and friends.

The Objibwa claimed that the Windego caused spiritual sickness, the worst type of illness that can afflict the living. Shamans or witch doctors who abused their psychic powers could be stricken by Windego sickness. The Objibwa also believed that a person who resorted to cannibalism was doomed to eternally wander the earth as a Windego, symbolically eating the dead. Many white settlers in the late nineteenth century reportedly saw the Windego as a death omen. The story of the Windego had spread quickly among new settlers when it was recorded by Jesse Nelson, a farmer living near Roseau, just south of the Canadian border. According to *The WPA Guide to Minnesota*, Jesse claimed he was "in the yard of the Mickinock house about mid-afternoon, looking south I saw that apparition rise by the muskeg and start walking westward . . . It was about fifteen feet tall, dressed in some material that looked like white lace. Whatever it might have been it was not a hallucination of superstitious fears in the dark for I saw it in broad daylight. Mrs. Mickinock died the following morning."

General interest in the legend of the Windego seems to have peaked around 1900. There have since been occasional, scattered reports of Windego sightings over the years by both Native Americans and others in Minnesota. These are followed inevitably by death.

The Phantoms of the Phoenix

Maybe they should have changed the name from Chisholm to Phoenix. It would have been appropriate. In Egyptian mythology, the phoenix is a symbol of rebirth, specifically rebirth through fire. The legend is that the aging phoenix bird, losing its strength and vitality, throws itself into a fire and is consumed. From the ashes arises a new, vigorous phoenix. That's pretty much what happened to the town of Chisholm in September of 1908.

Today, there are many good reasons to visit Chisholm, among them the Minnesota Discovery Center and the Minnesota Museum of Mining. A lesser-known entertainment is the chance to hear, even see, the happy ghosts of Chisholm's long-gone saloons, the New Chance and the Iron House. While many apparitions are gruesome or fearsome, the phantoms of the customers, bartenders, and entertainers of these saloons are not at all scary. They are a jovial lot, raising their glasses to toast the rebirth of Chisholm.

The iron-mining town of Chisholm was but seven years old when the fire struck on Saturday, September 5. It had been a hot, dry summer. Several small forest fires had earlier broken out near Chisholm, but the town's citizens hoped that its location on Long Year Lake would help to protect the town from disaster. They were wrong. The wind shifted direction suddenly and increased in speed. Fire swept down upon the town of six thousand people, forcing them to flee for their lives. The flames raced through town so swiftly that most folks ran for safety without even taking their cash and jewelry. Buildings literally exploded in the intense heat. Chisholm's citizens began running down the road toward Hibbing, the nearest town. The mass evacuation took place without the loss of a single life. The Great Northern Railroad, alerted by telegraph, sent a special fifteen-car train to take people to Hibbing, where a tent city was set up.

Only three buildings in Chisholm remained standing after the fire: two churches and the Last Chance Saloon. By Monday, September 7, the Last Chance, renamed the New Chance, was open for business, and business was good. Another saloon was created when an enterprising citizen placed a few planks across two barrels and announced that his new saloon, the Iron House, was open for business. The first freight train that Monday delivered lumber and other building supplies, along with eighteen barrels of beer. Rebuilding was a thirst-inducing business.

The merry ghosts of the New Chance and the Iron House usually manifest themselves as sounds. Along otherwise quiet, almost deserted downtown streets in the early-morning hours, the faint sounds of a piano playing ragtime music can be heard, along with laughter and the clinking of glasses. On those occasions when the ghosts can be seen, many colorful characters can be spotted. Burly bartenders in red vests and walrus mustaches serve up foaming mugs of beer. Dancehall girls in scarlet corsets and black fishnet stockings circulate among drunken miners. Toasts are offered and glasses are raised. The supernatural merriment seems contagious—those among the living who've witnessed the ghostly festivities cannot help smiling. Even if you don't actually hear or see these spirits, you might raise a glass to salute the spirited spirits of Minnesota's own phoenix.

The Spirits of Spirit Island

Their names are lost to history but their story will sound a little familiar. The couple could be called Minnesota's own Romeo and Juliet, for their love led to their deaths, just as in Shakespeare's immortal tale. Or maybe it didn't, for there are several versions about what happened on Spirit Island many centuries ago.

The theme of two young lovers ultimately doomed because their families, tribes, or nations were historic enemies shows up in virtually every culture around the world. The awesome power of true love and young passion reaches across the chasm of hate and mistrust between different races, ethnic groups, languages, and religions, successfully uniting the lovers but igniting wars between their families. It is an old story and frequently ends badly. Often, blood is spilled and animosities further strengthened.

Minnesota's own Romeo and Juliet saga played out on Spirit Island in Spirit Lake, just west of downtown Duluth. According to legend, the story is not over with; the doomed lovers' spirits still struggle to live together in peace and love, unable to overcome their tribes' mutual hostility.

According to legend, he was the son of a Sioux chief; she was a Chippewa princess. The Sioux, more properly called the Dakota, once had dominated the middle of the continent. They long had been under pressure from the Chippewa, who were one of the Algonquin peoples, a different language and cultural group who ruled the northeast region. The Sioux and the Chippewa were about as different as they could be, and the Chippewa persistently pushed west into traditional Sioux territory.

How the couple met is not recorded but apparently it was love at first sight. When they announced to their families their intention to marry, all of the mutual hatreds and suspicions boiled up, focused on the would-be couple. The Sioux chief told his son that the tribe could not allow such a disgrace to occur and that the young man would commit treason against his people by marrying the daughter of their bitter enemies. The Chippewa princess was warned that her own people would sooner see her dead than defiled by a Sioux. Understandably, the young lovers fled to a then-uninhabited place, Spirit Island. The island would be their refuge from their mutually hostile tribes.

Inevitably, both the Sioux and the Chippewa learned about the Spirit Island hideout. Both tribes determined to storm the island and exact vengeance; if both lovers were killed in the attack, then so be it. Death before dishonor was the determination of both tribes. Both the Chippewa and Sioux soon came to believe that the Spirit Island refuge of the lovers had some supernatural protection. Huge bears appeared along the shores of the lake. They stood up on their hind legs, growling threateningly. Arrows couldn't kill them. The warriors of both tribes had to retreat. Next, the Sioux and Chippewa camps were encircled by packs of wolves whose eyes and fangs glowed with greenish light in the nighttime darkness. Like the bears, the otherworldly wolves were impervious to human weapons. When some warriors managed to launch canoes on Spirit Lake with the aim of attacking Spirit Island, storm clouds appeared suddenly in a previously clear sky and the canoes were swamped by huge waves.

When at long last members of both tribes managed to get onto Spirit Island, they were astonished at what they found—or didn't find. There was absolutely no trace of the runaway lovers. They could not have escaped the Sioux and Chippewa who had ringed the shores of Spirit Lake, but somehow they had.

Then the haunting began. Minnesota's own Romeo and Juliet have materialized mysteriously over the years since their disappearance from the world of the living. Sometimes they seem to be normal, living beings, only to vanish as soon as the observer looks away for a moment. Many times, they appear as misty wraiths, almost transparent, at dawn or dusk. A few witnesses claim to have seen the couple, hand in hand, literally walking on water on Spirit Lake. The expressions on the faces of these ghosts, always seen together, are of joy in one another's presence. They are said to be focused on each other. Their love, which overcame such great obstacles, has become eternal in the spirit world. Their love conquered hate, mistrust, and deep prejudice; now it survives death itself.

The Turtle and the Snake

The turtle and the snake are haunted, according to old Native American traditions and continuing sightings over the centuries. This turtle and snake are easy enough to find, especially from the air, as they are Indian mounds built on the shores of Cut Foot Sioux Lake. The turtle is twenty-five feet wide and thirty feet long; the snake, built soon after the turtle, completely encircles the other animal. These mounds are monuments to war; they celebrate bloodshed and they are said to be haunted by the spirits of those who died on this spot.

Indian mounds, built painstakingly by piling up earth one basketful at a time, are very common throughout the Mississippi and Ohio Valleys. Many explanations are offered for their creation. Often, they were used as tombs for the burial of chiefs and other notables, similar to the pyramids built by the ancient Egyptians and Maya. These burial mounds were often conical or rounded pyramids. Very large mounds, such as Monk's Mound east of St. Louis, were truncated pyramids built as ceremonial platforms. Effigy mounds, depicting living creatures, also are common; the most frequent symbol is that of a snake. These effigy mounds, which are most easily identified and appreciated from an aerial perspective, are thought by some to have been built to communicate with either the gods or visitors from outer space. Why would effigy mounds, which are difficult to identify at ground level, be built if not to be seen from the heavens?

In 1748, a major battle was fought between the invading Chippewa and the defending Sioux. The Chippewa were soundly defeated and forced to retreat back to the north. The Sioux celebrated their victory by building the turtle mound. The turtle's head pointed north, the direction from which the invading Chippewa had arrived and in which they had been forced to withdraw. The giant turtle may have been used as an honored tomb for fallen Sioux warriors.

The Sioux triumph didn't last long. The Chippewa returned in force in a ferocious counterattack. The defending Sioux were surrounded and annihilated. Sioux warriors were beheaded, according to legend, and their women and children massacred. The morning after the battle, a group of Chippewa women found an unconscious Sioux warrior on the lakeshore. His foot had been nearly severed. They killed him and named the lake the Cut Foot Sioux Lake.

To celebrate their overwhelming victory, the Chippewa built a snake-shaped mound surrounding the Sioux's turtle. The snake's encirclement of the turtle symbolized the Chippewa's great victory over their Sioux enemies. The snake's head pointed south into Sioux territory—a pictorial threat of further Chippewa incursions into the Sioux's traditional hunting grounds. The snake may have been used as a collective tomb for Chippewa who fell in battle, so that the ultimately victorious Chippewa, in death as in life, surrounded their foes.

Allegedly, a battle scene is repeated over and over again on misty mornings: The phantom warriors from both tribes seem to rise up from the earth atop the turtle and the snake. After volleys of arrows cut down scores on both sides, the braves charge into one another's ranks, swinging war clubs and axes in bloody hand-to-hand combat. No quarter is given, no mercy expected or granted. This is war at its most ferocious. Two nations, deadly enemies for centuries, fight for control over fertile land rich with game. At least in the spirit realm, the fight goes on to this day.

Ironically, neither the Sioux nor the Chippewa warriors who fought and died in 1748 had any way of knowing that, within a century, both tribes would be witnessing a massive invasion of white settlers, one that ultimately would destroy their way of life. In a sense both the turtle and the snake now are imbedded in another conquering culture, as are the living descendents of the dead who are buried in the effigy mounds.

Wind Chimes

Almost always, Grandma got her way. Her wishes got fulfilled, her wants were satisfied, her opinions prevailed—at least in her own home, which was as it should be, in the oft-expressed opinion of Grandma. Not that the old lady was some obnoxious tyrant. Her strong opinions, firmly expressed, were well reasoned and tempered with consideration of others and love for her family. She was right much more often than she ever was wrong. Her advice was gold and her generosity legend. It's just that you didn't ignore Grandma or her wishes and that continued even after Grandma went to that big bingo game in the sky.

Grandma's greatest pleasure in life was hosting holiday feasts for her large family. She was a great cook, a most gracious and accommodating hostess. A firm rule, which grandchildren and, in turn, great-grandchildren learned early, was that no one messed with Grandma's wind chimes. She was tolerant of some exuberant behavior among children, but be careful around her wind chimes. Family history included one dark episode, long ago, when careless horseplay had resulted in the destruction of a particularly fragile set of painted glass chimes.

By coincidence, Grandma's death was shortly followed by the wedding of her youngest granddaughter. The family agreed that Grandma's house, in a suburb of Duluth, would be kept off the market until prices improved and that it would be rented to the newlyweds at reasonable rates.

Tinkle, tinkle went the delicate glass wind chimes, accompanied by the rapid clinks of the bamboo rods. The hollow clucks of the pottery figures as they clashed was in contrast to the muted clangs of the metal rods of yet more sets of suspended chimes. Bong, bong went the heavier brass bells when the wind currents were strong enough on the sheltered porch where the sturdier wind chimes were hung. What at first had seemed to be charming little sounds were becoming an unwanted cacophony of noise whenever the lake breeze picked up.

As time went on, breezes were no longer necessary to produce the wind chime symphonies. The noise was becoming more than just annoying, it was scary. The most fragile chimes were hung in the dining room, safe from any strong winds that might damage them. These chimes began sounding their ranges of notes as though a child was practicing the scales on a musical instrument. This was happening when no discernable air currents were moving.

The granddaughter remembered Grandma's habit of gently brushing hanging chimes with her fingertips as she walked by, just to hear the musical notes. Was Grandma's spirit still caressing her wind chime collection? The granddaughter carefully wrapped and packed away the chimes, exiling them to the attic. She was awakened the next morning by a wind chime concerto when all of the collection had mysteriously reappeared in their accustomed places. The granddaughter felt as though she had been mildly but firmly chastised for messing with Grandma's collection.

A family conclave decided to distribute the wind chimes among all the family households. One or two sets of chimes per house wouldn't produce overwhelming noises. The gentle sounds would remind everyone of Grandma's abiding love for them—as well as her strong will.

Southern Minnesota

THE SOUTHERN TIER OF MINNESOTA IS BOUNDED BY WISCONSIN, IOWA, South Dakota, and a line running east-west from the Mississippi River at Point Douglas due westward. Important towns in the region include Rochester, Mankato, New Ulm, and Winona.

Notable ghosts of this geographic area include the victims of a horrific steamboat explosion on the Mississippi River and the spirits of those killed in a famous bank robbery that became a gunfight. You'll hear about a ghost that became the talk of the town as well as phantoms said to haunt a pioneer mill, a theater, and a quarry valued by Indians. UFOs make several appearances and in one case transform a gentle pet.

Be Prepared

"Be Prepared" is famous as the motto of the Boy Scouts; it is also very good advice in general. Being prepared is a key to success and, often, a prerequisite to survival. Not being prepared in life doubtless has produced many ghosts, including the angry phantoms of Rollingstone City.

There is a small town called Rollingstone on the heights northwest of Winona, but this is a later creation unrelated to the Rollingstone City that attracted hundreds of doomed settlers back in 1852.

That Rollingstone existed only on paper and in the hopes and dreams of its promoters and the imagination of a gifted artist.

The 1850s were a time of rapid expansion of settlement in the Minnesota Territory, which had been created by Congress in 1849. The first territorial legislature convened at St. Paul that year; the 1850 census recorded 6,077 non-Indian inhabitants in the territory. Only seven years later, the population was over 150,000, and statehood was granted in 1858. Minnesota was booming, and most of the new arrivals achieved success. Rollingstone City was a tragic exception.

An association of New York City mechanics decided that wheat farming in Minnesota would be a profitable venture for their members. They dreamed of a better life on the beckoning frontier; they would apply for free government land and life would be good. An advance committee was sent west to select a site. Unfortunately, the committee members scored high on optimism but had no knowledge or experience in geography or agriculture. They mistook a shallow, unnavigable, almost stagnant side channel of the Mississippi for the main stream, and envisioned it as the site of their planned utopian city.

Back in New York, the well-meaning but clueless committee hired an artist to draw a picture of what the planned city of Rollingstone would look like. Wide, paved avenues radiated from a central business district filled with three-story stone and brick commercial buildings. A dozen steamboats were berthed at the waterfront. A magnificent opera house stood next to the dignified courthouse and city hall. Elegant villas lined the residential areas and parks were everywhere, complete with bandstands and athletic fields. It was a vision to die for; unfortunately, many members of the ill-fated colony did just that.

Somehow, the artist's idealized image of what the city would look like in the future was accepted by many as a view of what already existed. Excited association members drew lots for in-town house sites and outlying farms. They set off with unrealistic hopes and no knowledge of farming. At Mississippi River ports in Illinois, they tried to buy tickets to Rollingstone City, only to be told that no such place existed. When the settlers neared the map coordinates shown on their land deeds, steamboat captains dropped them off on the banks of the main channel, from which they had to haul their goods across the mudflats and back channels to the site of their imagined city.

Four hundred settlers huddled together in a few flimsy tents and log lean-tos covered in sod. Their eastern-made plows could not pierce the prairie sod; their food supplies ran out. They were not prepared for the brutal blizzards of an upper Midwest winter. The utopian city that never was and never would be became a graveyard. A few survivors moved to nearby Winona, while others found their way back to New York.

The ghosts of the never-was city of Rollingstone are consumed by the very worst kind of anger. They are angry at themselves for not being prepared. Being prepared is, quite literally, vital. The embittered ghosts of Rollingstone City were not, and paid the price of ignorance.

Examined by a UFO

Like most small towns, Worthington has a well-known, if unofficial, lovers lane, in this case a semi-secluded stretch of lakeshore on Lake Okabena. On summer days, the bathing beach and picnic tables host frolicking families. Evenings feature different kinds of frolics in the intimate privacy of parked cars. A pair of teenagers, whom we'll call Jack and Louise, had been looking forward to a few hours together in Jack's parents' car in the spring of 1958. The carefully planned cover story was that they had gone to a movie theater. They had discussed a review of the film printed in the local paper, so that they could answer any questions about it. The evening was rather on the cold side, but the car, like most Minnesota vehicles, was equipped with old blankets.

UFO sightings had been cropping up randomly across the country and the calendar that year, not that Jack or Louise was particularly interested or concerned. They were completely absorbed in one another. The car radio softly played Frank Sinatra; all was well with the world. The couple were entwined cozily, intent on moving on to further delights, when they became aware of a low humming, almost throbbing sound, similar to the sensation of passing beneath high-tension transmission lines. As though near a strong electrical field, they could feel the fine hairs on their arms seem to rise. The sound grew louder and appeared to come from directly overhead.

By now, it seemed as though the fillings in their teeth were vibrating, as they said later. The sound was actually shaking the car. Then a brilliant, purple light suddenly beamed down on them. Jack and Louise each fell into a dreamlike trance. They later related identical dreams to each other. The powerful light that filled their car gradually became a warm, viscous liquid that enveloped them completely. They had no sensation of drowning or difficulty in breathing. Afterwards, their clothing, hair, and the car's interior were perfectly dry.

After what seemed like hours but what must have been but a moment, the light faded to total darkness. The insistent noise likewise went away. As full consciousness returned, they glanced at the nearest other car, about sixty feet away. There was no indication that anyone else had noticed, or was aware of, their eerie ordeal. They did notice a faint, chemical odor, as though their clothing and the car's upholstery had just been dry-cleaned. Oddly, the car's interior appeared to have been vacuumed, it was so pristine. The candy bars brought by Jack as a little treat were gone.

Louise and Jack resolved to tell no one, especially not their parents, of their experience. They weren't supposed to be at the lover's lane. Who would believe them anyhow? To this day, they believe that they were the subjects of a non-invasive examination by the life forms operating a UFO. Life forms with a sweet tooth.

Goodbye to the Goodhue Ghost

Have you ever seen a ghost? Do you personally know anyone who has seen a ghost? A study conducted by the University of Chicago found that forty-two percent of adult Americans reported having had some type of contact with the dead. Perhaps "admitted" would be a better word than "reported." Other than in an anonymous survey, many people who believe that they have seen, heard, or sensed a phantom will not admit such contact except to a very limited number of their closest confidants. Few seek the disdainful disbelief, even mockery, of skeptical neighbors and associates. In a great majority of instances, the ghost is that of a relative or close friend; two out of three widows for example, believe that their dead spouses have reached out to them from beyond the grave.

On occasion, a public report of an apparition is followed by a flurry of similar sightings. True believers would cite these multiple, repeating experiences as proof that, yes indeed, there are ghosts. Psychologists might begin muttering about mass hysteria. More open-minded folks might conclude that many encounters with the supernatural that normally would have gone unreported now are openly admitted by persons emboldened by the public disclosure of others' similar experiences. Thus, one ghost story leads to another and yet another. It is easier to say. "Yes, I saw it too!" than to proclaim, "You won't believe what happened to me!" Judge for yourself the rash of ghost sightings in Goodhue.

To say that Goodhue is a small town is like saying that mosquitoes are on the small side compared to gorillas. What happens in Goodhue might stay in Goodhue, but everyone there will know of it, and quickly.

It was the early fall of 1922. Young Tom Wilson was walking past the apple orchard next to Holy Trinity Church and its graveyard. It was late; Tom had been calling on the future Mrs. Wilson and he was in a happy mood. Tom was whistling as he strolled along, but that ended abruptly when he realized that someone, or something, was walking just behind him, keeping pace. He could hear the footsteps but couldn't see anyone. Although it was a warm evening, Tom felt an icy breath on the back of his neck. Don't panic, he told himself, it's just your imagination. Tom soon found himself running at a flat-out sprint. The exhausted Tom ran all the way to the town marshal's house, where he breathlessly reported the unnerving experience. Tom's evident terror persuaded the marshal to accompany him as he retraced his route back to the orchard. Nothing was found.

The story soon reached the ears of everyone in town. Tom had to endure a good deal of good-natured teasing about the event. The next night, Bob Taylor was walking his dog near the churchyard. A blood-chilling scream was heard. The dog, a powerfully built German shepherd, laid his ears back flat on his head and took off like a Fourth of July rocket. Bob ran like he'd never run before. He and his dog were found hours later, both them of them lying flat on the ground covered in cold sweat and both whimpering quietly.

After the second incident, two mischievous cousins, both ten years old, decided to hide in the graveyard at sundown and watch for the ghost. A few hours later, their frantic parents went out looking for them and found the boys seated under a large tree, sobbing and staring at the full moon. Neither could speak for a full twenty-four hours; when their powers of speech finally returned, neither would talk about their experience. A year went by before either would go outdoors after dusk.

By now, the entire population was fearful of whatever it was that had frightened so many folks. The church's pastor teamed up with the town marshal. They decided to camp out in the orchard next to the graveyard. The marshal brought along his Colt Peacemaker and the pastor showed up with a large wooden cross used in church processions. Around midnight, both men had dozed off, but both awakened suddenly as a freezing fog enveloped them—most unusual in mid-September, even in Minnesota. A pulsating bright light in the shape of a huge wolf approached them. The pastor held his cross up and the marshal fired several shots at it. There was one loud yelp of pain, followed by silence. The strange light disappeared. Oddly, the wooden cross was singed and charred around the edges, as though brushed with fire. The Goodhue ghost was never reported again, possibly because for two generations, no one ever went near the area again.

Ghostus Maximus

Other folks might boast about their courageous watchdogs. Ellen was protected by a sagacious cat. Ellen was sure that Max remained on duty, even though Max's ashes were encased in a tasteful enameled brass urn on the mantelpiece. On occasion, Ellen could hear the cat's deep, threatening growl. Those supernatural growls warned her, as they always had, of some sort of evil. Max sensed evil intent and warned his mistress to beware, to avoid, to question.

Max came into Ellen's life at a time when each really needed the other. Max's mother, who had belonged to a friend of Ellen, had died soon after birthing her litter. Ellen agreed to bottle-feed the tiny, helpless kitten. She had been considering getting a pet to relieve her profound loneliness following the death of her husband of forty years. She needed, as she said, another heart beating in her home. She named him Maximus, which she believed meant "the most" in Latin. Maximus was the most adorable, most affectionate, smartest cat she'd ever known. She and little Max bonded well. Max's early kittenhood was spent in a basket lined with soft, old towels, which Ellen carried around with her.

The growing kitten soon demonstrated his strong instinct to protect his foster mother and benefactor. Whenever another person appeared in his home, Max would subject them to a thorough screening worthy of airport security on red alert. He would look them up and down, sniff deeply, and carefully observe their reactions to him. Any seated visitor soon had a lapful of boldly inquisitive cat whether they welcomed this or not. On occasion, Mac would stand in the visitors' laps, brace his front paws on their chests, and stare directly into their faces. Most visitors found this a tad intimidating. Then, Max would deliver his verdict. If the stranger was acceptable, Max would jump down and resume his nap. If Max curled up, purring, in the guest's lap, this was the ultimate "Maximus seal of approval," as Ellen would say. However, should the intruder set off Max's alarm system, the cat would arch his back, sink his claws into the offending person, and emit a piercing yowl. Most potential troublemakers promptly left.

Normally, life was uneventful in placid Redwood Falls, but evil has a way of showing up everywhere. Ellen's paperboy was a case in point. Max had taken an instant dislike to the boy and growled menacingly when the lad came to collect his money every week. Once, when the boy stepped into the house, he unwisely stooped to pet Max, who promptly bit his hand. When it was revealed that the boy had begun attacking younger children after practicing on the torture-murders of small animals, most folks were surprised. "But he was such a quiet, polite young man," was repeated for television cameras. Ellen, of course, realized that Max's negative reaction was exactly correct. She began to pay more attention to Max's feline intuition.

Max literally jumped into the roles of personnel administrator and social director. Candidates for doing yardwork, plumbing repairs, and cleaning lady were "interviewed" by Sir Max, and only hired on his approval. Acquaintances were invited to Ellen's house for tea and Max's examination before becoming trusted friends.

Max was hit and killed by a speeding truck right in front of Ellen's house. The cat had been uncharacteristically incautious in pursuit of love. Max's ashes had only recently been installed in a place of honor when Ellen began to hear his purrs of approval and his growls of warning again. Max is still on duty and you'd better listen.

The Haunted Mill

They used to tell this story in Minnesota Lake, a small town on the lake of that name about twenty miles south of Mankato. Few people now remember the tale of the cursed mill that killed its builder and owner. The miller himself believed that the mill was haunted by the Devil in person. Some folks in the neighborhood think that the miller was right.

The mill was so well constructed that it survived its builder by several decades despite being completely abandoned and neglected. No one was courageous enough, or stupid enough, to enter it. Still, on moonlit nights, some people claim to have seen the long-gone sails of the windmill turning slowly, even if there is no wind. More believe they've heard the clanking and grinding noises of the mill at work.

As happens often, the miller's most positive attributes were also, when carried to extremes, his curse and the causes of his downfall. He was undoubtedly hardworking, thrifty, ingenious, and ambitious. But he also was stubborn, unloving, and self-centered. He put his work ahead of personal relationships. His heart, observed his wife, was every bit as hard and cold as his grindstones, which, incidentally, were where his heart ended up.

Gottlieb Shastag came to Minnesota just after the Civil War. He had been a flour miller back in Holland and had ambitions to build and operate his own windmill. The perfectionist decided to build a Dutch-style windmill that would be the finest example of its kind. Shastag is said to have spent two years building his mill. Everything was made twice as large and strong as in an average windmill. He felled the trees himself, sawed the lumber, and hand-tooled the mill's machinery. Some gear wheels were ten feet in diameter. The main driveshaft was the entire trunk of a great oak tree. The four sails, or blades, of the windmill were thirty-five feet long. Just as was done back in Holland, the whole upper part of the windmill could be turned in any direction to face the wind. Gottlieb personally quarried and cut the huge grindstones. The mill had four doors, as the giant fan blades, sweeping close to the ground, could kill a person who was unwary of them as they rotated. Eventually, they did just that. Twice.

Gottlieb's mill was a big success. He seemed to be at work almost constantly, as was his mill. One day he was asked to look after his four-year-old son while his wife went into town to shop. While working that day, Gottlieb heard a strange sound in the mill and went inside to investigate. His son tried to follow just as the top of the mill swung around to face the wind. A rapidly moving blade struck the boy, decapitating him.

Gottlieb grudgingly agreed to attend the church service for his son, but refused to close down the mill, even for a day. "I can't let my business go to the devil just because there has been an accident," he said. His wife left him. He had no real friends, but people continued to do business with him because the price was right.

Everything began to go wrong with the mill. The machinery began to break down. The roof leaked. Large timbers snapped like matchsticks. Sometimes the grindstones would not turn. Some batches of flour turned sour and moldy overnight. Blood mysteriously contaminated the flour. Strange blue or green lights appeared around the mill at night. The miller swore that Satan himself was haunting his mill. Whatever could go wrong did go wrong. Farmers stopped bringing their grain to Gottlieb.

Finally, Gottlieb, by this time an old and bitter man, began living in his mill. His house had been sold to pay creditors. He could barely eat or sleep. He claimed that the Devil, in the form of a large black rat, was watching him all the time. On the fiftieth anniversary of his son's death, he heard the boy's voice crying out to him. Gottlieb rushed out the door of the mill, unheedful of the turning blades, which struck him and threw him back into the mill and into the grinding stones. In minutes, he was ground into a bloody puree. The grindstones never turned again. The windmill's sails still caught the wind, clattering away until the old mill at last burned down. Some believe that the huge blades can still be heard late at night, grinding away at the devil's work.

The Haunted Theater

The "old couple," as they are known, appear to really enjoy the theater in both senses—they appreciate live performances and they bask in the grand and romantic ambiance of the magnificent old building. They can be counted upon to be there early for the special performances for which the theater is noted. The old couple usually is the last to leave, if, indeed, they ever do leave. The old couple also is the odd couple, for they are there only in the supernatural sense. They are ghosts.

The old couple is careful never to detract in any way from the other theatergoers' enjoyment of the show. If the section of the seats they've chosen starts to fill up, they simply disappear. They seldom interact with the living. When spoken to, their only response is a polite smile, followed by a little wave of the hand as though greeting someone just behind the speaker. As the speaker turns to see the object of the old couple's attention, the pair fades into oblivion.

The two old theatergoers are distinguished by their rather formal, old-fashioned dress. It is assumed that they are of the same vintage as the theater, which dates to 1929. He is described as an elderly gentleman, dressed in a three-piece suit of striped gray flannel. His blue and gold silk tie is held in place by a silver-rimmed tiepin of iridescent abalone shell. His partner wears a knee-length white dress covered in tiny silver and blue glass beads. The old couple seldom are seen apart, though some claim to have spotted the man outside during intermission, smoking a large cigar.

Among the several other ghosts alleged to haunt Austin's historic Paramount Theater is the phantom of a janitor, said to hang out in the building's large, dark basement. This ghost, in contrast to the silent old couple, is heard more than he is seen. This phantom evidently is frustrated by the old theater's notoriously contrary heating and plumbing systems. He can be heard, venting his disgust, in the furnace room. Apparently, he, or rather his spirit, has an awesome vocabulary of profanity and he is not a patient man. Evidently, according to ear-witnesses, it is necessary to threaten the furnace to coax it into working properly. Some of the living maintenance staff swear that a string of ghostly invective actually does produce better performance of the heating and cooling systems.

These interesting and non-aggressive ghosts (only the furnace is ever threatened) are believed to add to the mystique of the beautifully restored Paramount Theater. Unlike most contemporary multiplexes in or near suburban malls, the Paramount was designed to lure patrons with its flamboyant luxury and exotic atmosphere. While many modern cinemas have all the ambiance of cinderblock shoeboxes, the Paramount was designed to provide the illusion of being in a Spanish courtyard. Theaters are all about illusions—maybe that's why so many are said to house ghosts.

The Phantom Steamboat

This truly extraordinary vision appears only during severe flood conditions on the Minnesota River. Fortunately for everyone, such catastrophic floods are a relative rarity, but they do occur, and so does the vision.

The sight of the phantom old-time sternwheeler is interesting in its own right. Painted white, with gold trim on the "gingerbread" decorative flourishes, the steamboat has two passenger decks topped with a small pilothouse towards the bow. Two black smokestacks with flared tops belch smoke as the steam engines power the stern paddlewheel. Blue uniformed soldiers line the rails, gripping tightly, their faces reflecting a mix of awe and fear. The cause for their ghostly concern is all too apparent. The steamboat is sailing sedately across flooded farm fields, a mile or more from the banks of the swollen river.

Observers blink twice. It is a double impossibility, a ghost boat performing an impossible feat. The fact is, however, that the real steamboat that produced this phantom actually did leave the Minnesota River's channel and sail right across flooded valley fields and meadows.

There is a theory that events that caused great emotional stress and physical trauma can leave a residue of paranormal energies behind. These energies, in turn, produce apparitions like the ghostly riverboat, recreating its epic journey.

The journey happened on April 9, 1861. The army had orders to move some troops from Fort Ridgely to St. Paul, about three hundred miles by riverboat. A federal agent chartered the sternwheeler

Fanny Harris to move the soldiers and their equipment. The Minnesota River was in flood, as snowmelt augmented heavy spring rains. The river had become a raging torrent. Bobbing along in the swift current were whole trees, fragments of houses and barns, and the carcasses of cows and buffalo. The surging river threatened to carry the *Fanny Harris* right into the banks of the many great looping swings of its channel. As the speed of the current exceeded the steamboat's top speed, the boat was not under control. It was a very dangerous situation.

The captain of the enormous boat decided that it would be considerably safer, as well as more direct, to leave the channel and, instead, sail across the flooded fields. Like all riverboats, *Fanny Harris* had been designed to travel in shallow water. She drew less than three feet and had a smooth, flat bottom. Her paddlewheel could actually push against the muddy surface of the drowned fields if necessary. Accordingly, the captain backed his boat against the northwest bank of the river near Belle Plain, warned everyone to hang on tightly, and opened the throttle. At full speed, the *Fanny Harris* charged the opposite bank, burst through the trees lining the riverside, and churned across ten miles of flooded flatlands before nosing back into the river.

The intense anxiety of everyone aboard the boat that boldly left the river is thought to have created a psychic whirlpool of trauma that manifests as a phantom during high-water times. Don't worry about the ghosts onboard the phantom riverboat. As with the original boat, everyone reached St. Paul safely, if a little shaken by their experience. By the way, the *Fanny Harris*'s speed record from Fort Ridgely to St. Paul was never broken.

The Pipestone Phantoms

The ghosts of Native American craftsmen bend over their work, intently focused on continuing their long tradition of carving the red stone into ceremonial pipes, also known as peace pipes. The quarry in which they work is an ancient one, in use for centuries before the advent of the whites. To the Plains Indians tribes, this was and remains sacred land, made holy by the blood of their ancestors. When smoked, the pipes carved of the soft, easily worked stone cemented the peace between formerly warring tribes. Only Native Americans have the right to carve the red pipestone.

Today, Omaha and Sioux artisans can be seen demonstrating their craft at the Upper Midwest Indian Cultural center at the Pipestone National Monument, located in Minnesota's southwestern corner. Congress created the national monument to preserve and protect the quarries that were so important to the cultural life and history of the tribes of the Great Plains. The pipestone is not just geologically unique. It also plays an important role in Native American mythology and legend.

In a legend common to both Omaha and Sioux peoples, Wahegela, the wife of a Yankton Sioux, was following a white buffalo, a powerful symbol of good luck and future prosperity. This mystical creature's hooves cut through the soil, revealing the red stone. The stone, according to ancient tradition, was colored by the blood of the first people—the ancestors of all Indians. Ancient hieroglyphs on the quarry walls recount the tradition that the Great Spirit created humankind on this spot. The hard red quartzite surrounding the softer pipestone is alleged to be the flesh of the first people, hardened by the waters of the Great Flood.

Since Wahegela was, by blood, an Omaha, that tribe claimed exclusive rights to her discovery. The Sioux claim was based on Wahegela's living among them for most of her life. The war over rights to the pipestone quarries continued for generations until it was decided at last that the pipestone area be declared neutral ground, available to any and all Plains Indians.

Are the phantom craftsmen, who appear only briefly in the early dawn light, the product of centuries of fervent prayers at the many shrines on this spot? Is the pipestone area actually a pool of psychic energy that attracts the phantoms of long-ago artisans? It is interesting that both Native Americans and Americans originating in Europe attach the same symbolic meaning to the color red. In Amerindian lore, red is the color of strong emotion, of courage and determination. The traditional explanation for the red in the American flag is that it signifies valor and fervor.

The early-morning ghosts of the pipestone carvers are not the only phantoms alleged to appear within the national monument's three hundred acres. A sheer pillar of blood-red quartzite is known as "leaping rock." An Indian maiden whose betrothed was killed in battle is said to have jumped off this pillar to her death. Her ghost is said to repeat this death leap at dusk on long summer nights.

The Shades of the Great Northfield Raid

If you would just as soon not meet some angry, frustrated ghosts armed with six-shooters, it would be best to avoid being in Northfield in early September, around the anniversary of the Great Northfield Raid. On the other hand, those interested in frontier folklore and the legendary outlaws Jesse and Frank James might choose to lounge about downtown in hopes of glimpsing the phantoms of the "seven minutes that shook Northfield." In those seven minutes, which started around 2 P.M. on September 7, 1876, a botched bank robbery became a battle that entered the history books.

Eight desperados attempted to rob the First National Bank on Bridge Square. Before the echoes of gunfire faded away, two bandits had been killed and one wounded, and two townspeople were dead and a third wounded. Northfield's citizens not only fought back, they actively pursued the robbers; by nightfall, the avenging posse numbered more than a thousand. They spent weeks searching an area of hundreds of square miles. You don't mess with Minnesotans.

The ghosts that are alleged to revisit Northfield near the anniversary of the raid may or may not include the phantoms of Jesse James and his brother Frank. It depends on which account you choose to believe. The James boys either successfully escaped the dragnet that caught the others, or they were never part of this raid. In his autobiography, written many years after the raid, Cole Younger of the infamous Younger boys claimed that the James brothers were not along on this bank robbery.

The raid was a total failure for the gang. Two bandits were killed on the streets of Northfield, and their ghosts are the ones described as writhing in agony in the street. A third robber was shot near Madelia, where the three Younger brothers surrendered. Robert Younger died in prison. James Younger committed suicide in a St. Paul hotel room after having been released from prison along with his brother Cole, who ended up running a Wild West show with Frank James. The total take from this bloody street fight was only $290.

Is there a difference between the spirits of the murderous thugs who carried out the raid and those of their innocent victims? Yes, claim some of those who, over the years, believe that they've witnessed these ghosts on the streets of Northfield.

The bank robbery had been planned well in advance, but for a different town. The gang had selected a bank in Mankato as their target. They studied the bank and memorized the layout, routines, and personnel. They familiarized themselves with the town's streets and a getaway route. As they showed up for their carefully rehearsed raid, they saw large crowds on the streets. Coincidentally, the local Board of Trade had staged a meeting that day to publicize their efforts to promote the town's business interests. The gang kept right on riding though town. They had no backup plan, and everything that followed was chaotic.

Once they arrived in Northfield, three robbers went inside the bank while the other five took up positions on the street outside to prevent anyone from entering the bank. Inside the bank, the robbers demanded that the safe be opened. No one would cooperate, so the gang shot the head teller, who happened to be the only one there at the time who knew the combination to the safe. A second bank teller was wounded while making his escape through the back door. Outside, a recent immigrant from Sweden was killed when he didn't respond to threats from gang members because he didn't understand English.

All of this gunfire didn't escape the notice of a pair of hardware store owners, who promptly handed out guns and ammo from their stock to the townspeople. It was as though a war had erupted in the middle of town.

It is said that, while the spirits of the bank teller and the innocent bystander are surrounded by a halo-like glowing fog, the ghostly forms of the dead robbers resemble disintegrating corpses, with black empty voids in the eye sockets. Some observers report a foul stench coming from the ghosts of the criminals. All in all, it might be a good idea to keep clear of the shades of the Great Northfield Raid.

The Shades of the Sea Wing Disaster

There is a great variety to ghosts, at least according to those who've seen or heard them. In many instances, the phantoms appear to be oblivious to the living, making no attempt to interact with those whose hearts still beat. Other spirits seem intent upon communicating across the chasm that separates the living from the dead, often selflessly attempting to warn the living of coming danger. And then there are the pathetic souls whose heartrending cries for help cannot be answered by the living, whose sympathetic impulses cannot rescue the doomed spirits replaying their last agonizing moments in this mortal sphere. Such is the case of the victims of the *Sea Wing* disaster.

The original tragedy played out on Lake Pepin on the evening of Sunday, July 13, 1890; the supernatural repetitions of the event have been observed on stormy summer evenings ever since, especially on the thirteenth day of the months of June, July, and August.

It had been a fun-filled day. Everyone was in a relaxed, happy mood. The 110-ton sternwheeler *Sea Wing*, based at Diamond Bluff, Wisconsin, had anticipated an overflow crowd that Sunday and towed a barge to accommodate extra passengers. The less-elegant facilities of the barge led to playful references to its being "second-class," but nothing could discourage the holiday atmosphere of the excursion. Families and friends of National Guardsmen from Minnesota's First Regiment were going to visit the soldiers encamped on the shore two miles south of Lake City. The regimental band provided music, games were played, people swam in the cool water, and everyone enjoyed a picnic lunch, along with a few cold beers.

Folks were reluctant to see the day end. The steam whistle of the *Sea Wing* had to repeatedly warn of the ship's departure as the tired picnickers straggled back aboard. The sky darkened quickly ahead of a storm sweeping in from the north. Very strong winds began propelling whitecaps across the lake. The ship's captain ordered that life preservers be handed out to all passengers but many did not bother to don them. Ninety-eight people, many of them children, had no clue that they were entering the final minutes of their existence. The other hundred or so people on the *Sea Wing* were about to survive a trauma that would haunt them for the rest of their lives.

Out of the menacing black clouds whirled a funnel-shaped vision of death. The tornado overturned the *Sea Wing* so suddenly that only twenty-five passengers were thrown clear into the churning black water. Most of these were able to climb up on the flat bottom of the steamboat. Those now trapped inside the hull began screaming and pounding on the hull, crazed with fear as the water level crept upwards toward their heads. Abruptly, violent winds turned the boat right side up briefly, throwing the survivors back into the water; the wind then overturned the boat a second time. The upside-down wreckage drifted to shore, accompanied by the barge which, oddly, was unscathed, losing not one of its terrified passengers.

One by one, the agonized cries of the struggling non-swimmers died away as they slipped beneath the waves. Gradually the frantic thumping from inside the upturned hull abated as the trapped air was used up.

The tornado dissipated and the rescue efforts began. The captain of a steamboat berthed at Lake City had to be rescued from a lynch mob when he refused to take his craft out on a storm-tossed lake to retrieve dead bodies. The *Sea Wing*'s captain had to be jailed in protective custody when he objected to holes being chopped in the overturned hull of his boat in order to extract the corpses.

To this day, the pounding sounds of those trapped in the *Sea Wing*'s hull can be heard echoing across the lake, accompanied by the forlorn cries of those about to drown. The ghosts of the ninety-eight victims of the *Sea Wing* disaster cannot rest quietly in their graves. It might be a good idea not to venture out on Lake Pepin after dark on the thirteenth day of a summer month.

The Spirits of the Condemned

The chants of these ghosts are faint now, a century and a half after the deaths of the Sioux warriors took place. Maybe what is heard is just the wind, gusty and bitterly cold, blustering into town from the north and west. The visual apparitions appear only briefly, and are almost transparent. As the eye registers the forms of the thirty-eight figures, they appear to dissolve in a swirl of dust driven by the shifting winds.

The brevity of the sight, however, cannot diminish the horror of the scene. Thirty-eight stalwart warriors, all in a row, are hanging from a gallows. Their heads hang limply from the thick ropes of the hangman's nooses. Their limbs twitch as life leaves their bodies but their eyes glow red in defiant stares that seem to penetrate the souls of observers.

This most unnerving sight is easily avoided by the faint-hearted—just stay away from the intersection of Front and Main Streets in downtown Mankato the day after Christmas. It was there that the largest public hanging ever to take place in the United States was carried out on December 26, 1862. It marked the conclusion of the bloody "Sioux Outbreak" that resulted in between four hundred and five hundred whites being killed by marauding Sioux warriors. The exact figure may never be known because many of the murdered lived on isolated farms and ranches.

Tensions between Minnesota's first inhabitants and white settlers had not been resolved by treaties signed in 1852. The Sioux probably did not fully comprehend the treaties; they had no conception of private ownership of land. The government's intention was to make farmers of the formerly nomadic Sioux, who instead wished to continue their dependence on hunting. Reservations had been established in the upper valley of the Minnesota River near Granite Falls and Redwood Falls. Although the reservations contained good farmland, the Sioux still preferred hunting to farming. The treaties also called for annual payments to the Sioux in the form of food and supplies. Dishonest traders routinely gave short weight, while some of the food was unfit to eat.

In 1857, a renegade band of Sioux killed thirty settlers in Iowa, and during their retreat north across Minnesota, killed several more settlers near Spirit Lake. No effort was made to capture and punish the band's leader, Inkpaduta, which convinced the Sioux that the federal government was toothless.

In the summer of 1862, the Sioux assembled at a government agency to claim their annual handout of food. Although food was in the warehouse, the agent refused to release it until the gold payment from Washington had arrived. The Civil War's demands for financing had delayed the gold. The Sioux were frustrated and angry. Four Indians who had been accused of stealing some eggs from a farmer killed five whites. In an all-night tribal conference, it was decided to go to war rather than wait for the whites to retaliate.

Fifteen hundred braves went on the attack. The Sioux were emboldened by their observation that many soldiers had been transferred back east to fight in the Civil War. This was the Sioux's best chance to defeat those who had taken their land. A stretch of the Minnesota River Valley, two hundred miles long and fifty miles wide, was laid waste by the marauding Sioux. Battles at Fort Ridgely, New Ulm, and Birch Cooley finally defeated the Indians and freed 269 white women and children captured as slaves. A military court tried 500 warriors; 303 were found guilty and condemned to death. President Lincoln commuted the sentences of all but those thirty-eight in whose cases there were eyewitness accounts of atrocities against unarmed civilians. The others, said Lincoln, must be treated as prisoners of war.

The thirty-eight condemned men were brought to the gallows platform. They requested that their chains be removed so that they could join their ancestors without shame. This was done. Singing war chants, each warrior placed the noose around his own neck. A man whose entire family had been murdered was given the honor of cutting the rope that sprung all the traps simultaneously.

Did the bravery with which those condemned faced death produce the ghosts who haunt their place of execution each anniversary of their death? Many believe so.

The UFO and the Guinea Pig

Louise was never the same again after the UFO incident. It totally changed her perception of danger and instilled in her a lifelong fear of UFOs. The event occurred way back in the 1970s, when Louise was in fourth grade and Chester was her favorite pet—at least until he was killed by a mysterious light beamed from a hovering spacecraft.

Chester came into Louise's life as a compromise. Louise's brothers were highly allergic to furry animals. Dogs and cats were out of the question, as much as Louise begged. She had goldfish, which were pretty but not exactly pets. How could you pet a fish? It was a friend of her parents who came up with the idea of a guinea pig. They were, he pointed out, docile and placid animals that never bit, unlike hamsters and gerbils. Louise's mother had previously ruled out pet mice or rats as she feared that they would escape and infest her house. A guinea pig, however, would be unadventurous and perfectly content to live in Louise's room, which was already off-limits to the brothers and their allergies.

Chester was a brown and white smoothcoat who was like a small lapdog without the bark. He was perfectly content to snuggle down in Louise's lap and be stroked lovingly. He lived in a series of cardboard boxes obtained from a supermarket in nearby Redwood Falls. When moved into a fresh box, the pig would chew a large hole in the side of the container—not as a means of escape but as a window so that the little creature could see what was going on. He would lean out his window and squeak his polite requests for food and attention. It was this habit that contributed to his final transformation.

Louise never will forget the night of the UFO. She was one of the very few who saw it, or at least were willing to admit that they saw it. It was a dark, overcast night in her rural neighborhood. Louise was in her room, supposedly doing her homework but really reading a book about vampires. The rest of her family was out shopping and it was just her and Chester in the house. Then Louise became aware of a faint humming or buzzing. She could feel the vibrations more than she could hear a sound.

The UFO appeared as a bright disk in the dark sky, like a silvery Frisbee. A strange greenish light projected from the underside of the craft, sweeping across the ground like a brilliant searchlight. Louise hid under her bed, something she hadn't done since she was four. Suddenly, the light shone into her bedroom window. Chester, ever curious, leaned out of his "window" and was quickly discovered by the roving light. Chester appeared to freeze as the light focused on him. His button eyes seemed to glow with an inner light. His body became wracked by a series of convulsions that ended only when the probing light blinked out and the UFO quickly disappeared in the northern sky.

Chester was uncharacteristically still for a few moments before shuddering one more time. He then died as Louise watched in horror. A large quantity of blood flowed out of his mouth as he expired.

Chester's burial took place in the backyard the following day. Louise wrapped his plump little body in an old dishtowel before placing it in the shoebox that would be his coffin. Curiously, the undoubtedly dead body should have been cold but it was hot, almost too hot to touch. For several years, no vegetation would grow atop Chester's gravesite.

Louise's recommendations concerning UFOs? Be afraid. Be very afraid. Curiosity is said to kill cats; it certainly proved lethal for guinea pigs.

Whispers and Whimpers

A couple we'll call Mary Jane and Bob Lewis had a brush with the supernatural that changed their beliefs about hauntings and ghosts. Although it had its scary moments, in the end their experience was more heartwarming than horrific.

"There's no such thing as ghosts," each had been reassured in childhood. "It's all make-believe. The stories might be interesting, but they're all made up or imagined by superstitious people, or folks who want attention." Both Bob and Mary Jane, proud of their college educations and their careers as teachers, had strong negative opinions about spirits and the occult. Until they moved into their retirement house, that is.

After both had retired from the Minneapolis schools, they decided to move out of the big city and relocate in their original hometown, Mankato. They found a 1950s split-level house in excellent condition. The price was right because the house had been on the market for more than a year. "The owner is motivated," they were told, which they knew was realtor-talk for "desperate."

They fell quickly into a routine that gave each some "private time." Bob liked to watch the financial news channel in the living room, while Mary Jane indulged her semi-secret passion for "soaps," as her mother had called them, on the second television in the family room. It was there that she encountered Keith, or rather, Keith's ghost.

Actually, it was OhBoy the cat who first was aware of Keith. OhBoy got his name because his endless curiosity led to many small mishaps. "Oh boy, what has he done now!" was such a frequent response to the cat's mischief that his name was changed from "George" to "OhBoy." From their first day in the house, the cat would not go into the smallest bedroom upstairs. Then, in the middle of Mary Jane's favorite soap, OhBoy had a fit. He arched his back, laid back his ears, hissed, and fled the room as though Satan himself was after him.

Mary Jane, who had been absorbed in the convoluted love life of the show's central character, was startled enough to turn off the sound on the TV. In the stillness she heard the sound of a small child's whimpering. It was a faint sobbing sound with barely intelligible words: "Mommy, mommy, I want my mommy." Mary Jane's emotions overcame her. She began sobbing herself. A very young child was in trouble and Mary Jane was sympathetic, but also terrified. "Mommy, I miss you. Where have you gone?" Bob heard it too, which reassured Mary Jane a little.

Every day it seemed the whimpering, whispering spirit made its presence known. The house wasn't theirs anymore, at least not theirs alone. Poor OhBoy seemed ill at ease all the time, interrupting his naps to cautiously patrol the house but consistently avoiding the smallest bedroom. Bob and Mary Jane had grown used to the pathetic whimpers and barely audible whispers when the ultimate scare occurred. The horrifying event led to their consulting a psychic.

If, a month earlier, someone had predicted that they would call on a psychic for help, they would have smiled condescendingly and smugly congratulated themselves on their rational intellects, safe from superstition and invulnerable to frauds. But now they were desperate. The spirit haunting their house was becoming more aggressive and more pathetic at the same time.

Bob was out running errands and Mary Jane had just settled in for a nap when she felt someone, or something, get into bed with her. The mattress sagged a little as though a weight had been added. She lay absolutely still, petrified by fear. She was lying on her side and her new, most unwelcome bed partner added not just weight but intense cold to her bed. It was as though a bag of ice had been laid against her spine. Her mouth gaped open in a soundless scream. It was as though her vocal cords were paralyzed. An all-too familiar childish voice whispered "Mommy? Mommy? I want my mommy."

Then, suddenly, the spirit left. Mary Jane was shaking violently, uncontrollably. She could hear and feel her heart pounding rapidly. This all must end. A friend of a friend knew of a psychic, who agreed to investigate the haunting. As the psychic requested, she was left alone in the house for twenty-four hours and was able to report success in contacting the whispering spirit. His name was Keith. He was almost four when he died in a car crash that also killed his father. Poor little Keith was unable to cope with becoming a spirit, wandering forlornly in a now-alien world. He finally found his way back home, only to find strangers living there.

The psychic also learned that Keith's mother had put the house up for sale and relocated closer to her parents in another town. The psychic was able to help Keith's spirit to migrate to his mother's subconscious mind, where Keith could become a series of short, pleasant memories or recurring dreams. With Keith's ghost gone, life became normal and tranquil again for Bob, Mary Jane, and OhBoy. Mary Jane, with OhBoy sleeping in her lap, resumed her routine watching her favorite soap.

Twin Cities
Metropolitan Area

THIS RELATIVELY SMALL REGION CONTAINS MINNEAPOLIS, MINNESOTA'S largest city, and the state capital, St. Paul, as well as their suburbs. In this region you will meet the ghosts of some of the state's important historic personages and the most famous racehorse of a century ago. You'll learn a history lesson from a ghost and meet a phantom adventuress who once sat on a queen's throne.

A History Lesson from a Ghost

Sam's interest in history was so intense that he earned a PhD in American history. He always credited his lifelong passion for understanding what happened, when and why to an early lesson in history taught by, or at least inspired by, a ghost.

Sam's family had made a tradition of visiting the family plot in an old St. Paul cemetery every Memorial Day. As a prelude to a backyard barbeque, the family would tidy up the family graves, plant new flowers, and place a new American flag atop the resting place of an uncle killed in the Korean War. As kids will do, Sam wandered over to a nearby section of the cemetery to look for interesting tombstones. He found something interesting all right: the barely visible, misty outline of a soldier dressed in a Civil War uniform. The phantom appeared to have a gruesome, gaping hole in his chest—the cause, no doubt, of his untimely death. Sam, paralyzed by shock and fear, stood rooted to the spot as the specter rose shakily to its feet and saluted the new American flag planted over a neighboring grave. In a startlingly clear, strong voice, the ghost said, "Eight in ten fell in ten minutes, but the Union was saved." With that sphinx-like pronouncement, the ghost faded away.

Sam was in a cold sweat. Surely he hadn't really seen a ghost. The voice he heard must have been in his head, the product of an overactive imagination. He didn't tell his family about this scary little adventure.

Sam eventually confided in his history teacher, downplaying the ghost part. "Why would a Civil War soldier say this?" Sam asked after repeating the phantom's words. Fortunately, this teacher was a Civil War buff. "The reference must be to the heroic charge of the First Minnesota Regiment at Gettysburg during the Civil War," the teacher explained. As Sam did more reading on this lead, he learned more about the First Minnesota's role in winning the crucial battle.

Historians agree that the turning point of the Civil War was the Battle of Gettysburg, which was the greatest battle, in terms both of casualties and consequences, ever fought on this continent. After Gettysburg, the South never again mounted a major offensive into Northern territory. A sound argument can be made that the 262 men and officers of the First Minnesota saved the Army of the Potomac from defeat, helping to win the battle and the war and preserve the Union.

Early on the morning of July 2, 1863, the battle's second day, the men of the First Minnesota were stationed behind the Union's front line as a reserve, ready to be brought into battle in any portion of the field where reinforcements were needed. They soon were needed. Confederate generals James Longstreet and A. P. Hill were leading a fierce attack; the heavy fighting forced Union commanders to continually move troops to the sectors with the most action, eventually creating a gap in the Union line. It looked as though the gap could be exploited, which might enable the Confederates to outflank the Federals and win the hard-fought struggle. More Union troops had been ordered to this portion of the line, but had not yet arrived. The First Minnesota, the only available unit near the gap, was ordered to charge toward the surging Confederates in order to buy time for reinforcements to arrive.

The Union line held, but the cost was high, especially for the First Minnesota. The 262 Minnesotans charged courageously into the advancing Confederates. Only forty-seven returned unscathed. The 215 who were killed or wounded in less than ten minutes represented a casualty rate of 82 percent, or roughly eight out of every ten in the regiment, just as the ghost said.

"Go back to the cemetery and look at the tombstone where the spirit appeared," the teacher advised Sam, "I'll bet the date of death is July 2, 1863." Sam returned to the cemetery and looked: the date was accurate, and the ghost's words were explained. It was one of the eight in ten who fell in ten minutes to save the Union. Ghosts can be very effective history teachers.

A Textbook Case

If Craig could have afforded a new textbook, none of this would have happened to him. Or if he'd chosen a different elective, or if he hadn't been accepted at the University of Minnesota, or if he'd never been born. Life had been so simple before he'd read that textbook, or, more specifically, before he'd learned to decipher its hidden messages. Those messages from beyond the grave predicted the future, and they were uncannily accurate and most disturbing. Foreknowledge could be a terrible burden. Especially if the future included death: who, when, how, and where, just as journalism students were taught to list, and just as Craig would have preferred not to know.

Craig Martin was a double major in political science and pre-law beginning his senior year when he acquired the cursed textbook. He had to pick up a social science elective outside his major and chose one that fit his usual requirements: mid-morning start time, in the same building as a preceding class, and, above all, not too challenging. His choice was world geography. How hard could that be, he thought—people learned geography back in fourth grade, right? One unexpected problem was that geography texts were quite pricey, so Craig bought a cheap used copy. Previous owners had used highlighters to underline what they thought was particularly important, meaning what they thought was a likely test question. Craig found this very annoying. Not only was it distracting, but did it even help? It would have been nice if the grades received by those who underlined were posted in front. The pages were a kaleido-scope of different colors, occasionally overlapping. The users of yellow and pink underliners, for example, both appeared fixated on statistics, which were now covered in a strange shade of orange. Craig considered the apparently random underlinings to be more ritual than analytical—the act of underlining served to reassure lazy students that, yes, they were taking this study stuff seriously.

It was the geography professor's sudden death that led to Craig's accidental discovery of the supernatural messages in the textbook. The man wasn't particularly old, and he looked healthy enough, but he collapsed during class one day, clutched his chest, groaned, and became very still after a spasm of twitching. That same evening, Craig noticed that, in addition to the rainbow of colored highlighters, someone had used a very fine black ballpoint pen to underline isolated words and letters. Without consciously thinking about it, Craig was suddenly aware that, right there in the discussion of Germany's role in the European economy, was the professor's full name and the statement that he would die of a heart attack on October 15 of that year. And that this would happen in class.

Craig forgot all about studying. No one had touched his book since the shocking death he had witnessed. With shaking hands, Craig opened the book again. Why hadn't he noticed the sporadic ballpoint underlining before? He'd been distracted by the colorful felt-tip markers. He backtracked to an earlier chapter and methodically picked out the message that Susan Smith was to die of an overdose of prescription pain pills on April 30 of the preceding year in her dorm room. He looked up the microfilmed copy of the campus newspaper for early May of the previous year. A lurid headline proclaimed the tragic event that stunned the university community. Now Craig remembered it. The name sounded familiar. It was inscribed on the inside cover of his textbook. Susan had been one of the previous owners. Had she read about her fate in this cursed book? Was her death an accident or was it suicide?

Craig didn't want to open the book again, but he couldn't resist. Early in the next chapter was a note that a mysterious fire would claim the lives of dozens of lab animals in the biology building on October 20 of that year—five days in the future. Craig waited nervously for those days to pass. The fire happened just as predicted. Another page predicted the death of his roommate's mother, right down to the time, place, and cause (a car crash). It happened, right on schedule.

When Craig worked up the nerve to open the book to the last chapter, he saw the coded notice that began, "On the day after his graduation from law school, local resident Craig Martin . . ." That was when he tossed the book into the fire. Some things about the future you really don't want to know.

Birdbrains

Jack had been afraid of his aunt's pet parrots since he was a little boy. It's not like they were obviously dangerous, hostile creatures; far from it. But it was the way the birds watched you—their heads swiveling, their whole bodies twisting to follow your every move. Their beady yellow and black eyes were expressionless, yet somehow they penetrated into one's soul. Jack didn't like them. He didn't trust them, and he was sure that the parrots knew he feared them and that they took some sneaky avian joy in this.

His Aunt Gloria had owned those two parrots for as long as he could remember. Whenever his parents had taken him to her house in Minneapolis for a visit, he had been warned to be on his very best behavior. "If Aunt Gloria likes you," they would remind him, "you could be a very rich little boy some day." As he grew older he more fully appreciated two facts: Aunt Gloria was really, really rich, and his poor parents were compulsively fixated on someday inheriting her money. Aunt Gloria was a childless widow and her only sister was intent on ensuring that she, or at least her own son, would inherit Gloria's clearly large estate. And so little Jack was encouraged, actually required, to please Aunt Gloria in every way possible. "Give your Aunt Gloria a big hug," they would say, "Give her the picture of flowers you drew with your crayons."

Visits to Aunt Gloria's house were ordeals for Jack. Not that his aunt was unpleasant. She always smiled at Jack and gave him nice presents and special treats. But Jack's parents would later smack his behind if he had failed to thank his aunt with sufficiently fulsome gratitude or, heaven forbid, smudged the image of the perfect little gentleman that they demanded he project. "And don't go near those damn parrots!" they would quite unnecessarily remind him. "They could bite you and cause a fuss and upset Aunt Gloria."

What unnerved Jack was that the big birds were not in cages. They were fastened to their perches by short lengths of chain connected to metal rings around one leg. Jack had never seen either one attempt to fly, but he had nightmarish visions of them lunging at him as he fearfully passed by.

The parrots talked, sometimes with amazing clarity. They were called Bill and Jill, though Jack could discern no difference between them. Jill could produce an uncannily accurate imitation of Gloria's laugh, a full-throated, hearty "ho, ho, ho." She could also mimic Gloria's voice, saying "Hello," "Thank you," and "Do you want a nut?" Bill would randomly repeat, again in Gloria's distinctive voice, "Goodbye now," "Here's a treat," and "What now?"

When Jack was nineteen, he lost both parents in a car crash. After funeral expenses and settling their debts, Jack found that he had inherited about two thousand dollars. Motivated by greed and laziness and unhindered by a conscience, Jack began to earnestly cultivate a close relationship with rich old Aunt Gloria. He visited often, flattering her with attention and listening sympathetically to her complaints about advancing age and her heart troubles. More than once he rushed to bring her the nitroglycerin tablets she would place under her tongue to ward off a potentially fatal heart attack. Slowly, Jack allowed himself to think about hiding those tiny pills. He knew he was Gloria's sole heir, so why not hasten the day when he would be a wealthy gentleman of leisure? He moved into Gloria's house so that "he could take better care" of dear old Auntie. When Gloria's heart next warned her of impending doom, Jack simply stood by with an evil smile.

Maybe Jack was not convincingly mourning Gloria's demise, but for whatever reason, the police detectives who came calling were not satisfied that this was an unassisted move into the next world. Jack blandly proclaimed his total innocence until the parrots interrupted. "Murderer!" screamed Bill, or was it Jill? "Jack murdered her," said the raucous parrot, "Murder!" Jack broke down and confessed all. He sobbed, overcome not by remorse, but by grief at being caught, by being ratted out by those damn birds. As he was led away in handcuffs, he heard "Goodbye now," accompanied by a parrot's version of Gloria's laugh.

"Boy, that was a surprise, him breaking down like that and confessing," remarked one of the detectives. "Guilty conscience," replied the other. "What should we do with these parrots?" he asked. "Well, I don't know," said his partner. "They must be pretty old. They haven't made a sound all the time we've been here."

Scientists claim that parrots simply mimic sounds, without comprehending any meaning to those sounds, hence the term, "birdbrains." Was it all in Jack's imagination? Or were the parrots channeling Gloria from beyond the grave?

Bits and Pieces

These particular ghosts have not been reported in recent decades, which is very good news for the sanity and general peace of mind of the fine citizens of Minneapolis. Of course, it could be that anyone who has encountered these horrifyingly gruesome apparitions was too traumatized to describe them to others. We protect ourselves from insanity by burying our most disturbing experiences deep in the subconscious. If ever terrible images deserved oblivion, it would be the visions of the phantoms of the victims of the great flour mill explosions of 1878.

In all probability, the stories of the fragmentary ghosts created by these historic explosions still live in the oral traditions of many Minneapolis families; at least one family's descendents were willing to retell their ancestor's account of what he termed "the bits and pieces."

A well-established theme in ghost stories of many cultures around the world is the powerful compulsion of the dead to reunite all of the fragments of their corpses in order to move on to the spirit world. Many a victim of violent dismemberment is alleged to wander the earth searching for that missing part before settling into the grave for the long sleep. The necessity of an intact, complete body in order to achieve eternal rest goes back at least to the mummies of ancient Egypt.

The terrible dilemma torturing the spirits of those killed in the Minneapolis flour mill disaster was that the corpses were blown into hundreds of tiny pieces, many no more than a fragment of soft tissue or splinter of bone. These phantoms were compelled to search every square inch of a large area of central Minneapolis. The odds of locating every shred of their former physical selves must have been dishearteningly small. These torn bits and pieces of once-living bodies would have been hidden in a matrix of shattered buildings and demolished equipment.

The eyewitness account of the "bits and pieces" phantoms searching for their missing parts remains as profoundly horrifying as it was four or five generations back. It was a bone-chilling sight. It was as though a miniature tornado or whirlwind had formed, a rotating column of bits and pieces of human being. This nightmarish ensemble moved, slowly and deliberately, over the utterly devastated ruins, pausing now and then to pull another shred of flesh into the rotating column of bloody remains. Transfixed, immobilized by this supernatural sight, the terrified observer carried this glimpse of hell, unforgettable in all its gory detail, to his grave only after confiding in his children. They in turn told the story to their mature children, and so the tale moved down the generations.

The event that produced the "bit and pieces" phantoms was the catastrophic destruction of the Washburn "A" Mill, which at the time was the largest flour mill in the world. In the 1870s, the Falls of St. Anthony supplied power to twelve mills producing a quarter million barrels of flour a year, one third of which was exported to Europe. Minnesota flour commanded a premium price and the mills grew ever larger, producing greater profits and greater dangers. Fine, powdery dust was everywhere in the flour mills, creating a permanent indoor fog of superfine wheat particles suspended in the air, very similar to the fine coal dust in underground mines. Such dust clouds were highly explosive. A spark could produce a catastrophic blast, which is precisely what happened at 7:10 P.M. on May 2, 1878. All fourteen workers in the mill at the time died instantly. Four others perished when two other mills, a machine shop, a woodworking plant, and a railroad roadhouse nearby were also reduced to dust. A ghastly rain of pulverized bodies, stone, brick, concrete, wood, and iron fell over many square blocks of the city. Windows were shattered for blocks around. Railcars were overturned. The entire roof of the Washburn Mill, weighing hundreds of tons, is said to have flown five hundred feet straight up in one piece, during which it cracked and fell in millions of pieces that mangled with other debris—including chunks of the eighteen victims.

Have all the scattered bits and pieces of those eighteen men been reunited in reasonably complete bodies? We can only pray so, for the sake of the victims and the mental health of potential eye-witnesses to their fragmented ghosts.

Happy Halloween

The family we'll call the Todds hadn't lived in their new neighborhood for long. Their move to the suburbs of Minneapolis had been timed to coincide with the beginning of a new school year for the kids, Kevin and Walt. The adult Todds had just begun to get to know their neighbors. Not that they weren't friendly, for they were, but all the adults in the neighborhood seemed to work out of the house, so social opportunities were few. Too bad, for the Todds hadn't heard all the neighborhood lore yet, and so didn't learn about the haunted house until Halloween.

The housing subdivision into which the Todds had moved dated to the 1960s, which explained the prevalence of "raised ranchers": three-bedroom ranch houses sitting atop a high basement containing a large family room, a den or bedroom, a half-bath, and a laundry room. Further south, closer to the city, were clusters of split-levels dating to the 1950s, mixed with Cape Cods from the 1940s.

Amid this standard suburban architecture, the Spanish-style house at the edge of the Todds' neighborhood stood out. Two stories tall, it had one-story wings flanking either side of the front entrance. The once-white stucco walls were rather gray now, stained here and there with mildew. The orange-red barrel tiles on the roof had faded to a soft rust color. A servant's apartment topped a separate three-car garage out back. The house's once-spacious grounds had been subdivided back in the mid-sixties. The "big house," as the neighborhood kids called it, sat sadly neglected. As the Todds, and everyone else, discovered later, the property was in legal limbo—a contested will from the last occupant had led to questions as to who was to benefit from its sale. The taxes were paid by the deceased's estate but no one looked after the house. Decades of unchecked growth of trees and shrubs had screened the house on all sides, producing an untidy little forest amidst neatly trimmed suburban house lots.

Like many of his contemporaries, the Todd children's father decided to accompany his offspring on their door-to-door candy quest, as the world seemed a little scarier place than it had in his own days of trick-or-treating. Mom stayed home to hand out candy bars.

The kids were having a great time. They noticed that the "big house," normally silent and dark, was all lit up. A noisy party seemed to be underway. Dad, curious about the sounds of merriment coming from the mysterious mansion, tagged along with the kids to the foot of the entrance walk.

What they saw was amazing. The whole house seemed to have come alive. Large jack o' lanterns were displayed in every window, flashing their trademark gap-toothed smiles. Every room was lit brilliantly, and it seemed that the untamed bushes that formerly blocked the windows had shrunk back. Someone with more enthusiasm than skill was pounding out Dixieland jazz on a piano, accompanied by loud laughter and the clinking of glasses. The front door stood open, giving a good view of tuxedoed men and women in short beaded dresses. It looked like an elaborate costume party with a "Roaring Twenties" theme. A beautiful young woman near the door noticed Kevin and Walt (a cowboy and a skeleton) standing there and presented each with a candied apple on a stick and a shiny coin. The kids thanked her nicely before continuing down the street and returning home.

That would have been the end of the story except that Walt and Kevin's mom mentioned to a neighbor the next morning that the "big house" was occupied again, and by very generous people too. The coins given to the boys turned out to be genuine silver dollars, in mint condition and dated 1924. As collectibles they were quite valuable. "But that can't be!" exclaimed the Todds' neighbor. "The big house was destroyed by fire at noon yesterday, before you were home from work and school."

Kevin and Walt still have those silver dollars—souvenirs of a Halloween they won't forget.

High-Definition Ghosts

The picture was bright, sharp and clear—magnificent, really. The fifty-inch screen was a little overwhelming in the relatively small room, but Jordan hoped she'd soon be moving into more spacious quarters. This splendid new flat-screen high-definition TV had been her present to herself after she had paid off her college loans and bought a very modest little car. Her late grandfather, whose legacy she had spent so conservatively, would have been proud of her. The trouble was that her grandfather's image was showing up on her new TV when the set was turned off. Unplugging the set didn't affect the image. Worse, the images of other dead people—relatives, friends, and acquaintances—kept appearing onscreen.

Jordan was not going crazy, at least she was pretty sure she wasn't. She reasoned that she couldn't be seeing dead people on her TV, but she was. The pictures of the deceased never conflicted with shows she was watching. It was after turning off her set that the dead appeared. Not that they looked dead. The images were usually smiling and animated, apparently trying to communicate with her, but no sound ever accompanied the pictures.

The images persisted. Jordan took to leaving the TV on at all times to avoid seeing the dead. She had been raised by parents who expressed skepticism about anything supernatural; she couldn't go to her family for any emotional support in dealing with these high-definition ghosts. A friend of a friend put her in touch with a psychic, whose analysis proved correct.

First of all, Jordan was lonely. She was far from home, living by herself in a small apartment near the state university campus in Minneapolis. She had focused her attention on her first job after graduating from the university, and her social life was almost non-existent. The psychic suggested that Jordan "saw" her grandfather on the TV screen because the set reminded her of her grandfather's kindness and his legacy that paid for her TV. Thinking about her deceased grandfather reminded her of her sense of loss.

Jordan, it turned out, had a strong spiritual side that she had subconsciously buried in order to conform to her parents' strongly negative views on ghosts and the supernatural. The psychic encouraged Jordan to explore her newly discovered abilities to communicate with the spirits of the dead. Jordan had been projecting her mental images of dead loved ones onto the blank screen of her TV. She learned to rechannel her sensitivity to the spirits—and she's now a recognized and successful psychic in the Twin Cities region.

In a Pig's Eye

This particular ghost is unforgettable, not that seeing any ghost wouldn't burn itself into one's memory. The appearance of this phantom seems to be associated with the consumption of large quantities of alcohol, which is appropriate, as the ghost is thought to be that of a notorious bootlegger and saloon keeper.

His name, he said, was Pierre Parrant and he was from Sault St. Marie, maybe. It was difficult to know exactly what to believe about this adventurer who arrived in Minnesota about 1830. People didn't call him Pierre Parrant anyhow, instead preferring to use his colorful nickname, Pig's Eye. In those days long before the rise of political correctness, physical handicaps or blemishes often became the basis of memorable, if demeaning, nicknames. Pierre had a blind eye, like a milky blue marble with a white ring around the pupil, giving a piggish expression to his ugly face, and thus he was dubbed "Pig's Eye."

Pig's Eye claimed to have been a Canadian voyageur, one of the adventurous fur trappers and traders who first explored the region. But it wasn't fur that attracted him to Minnesota—it was a different kind of business opportunity. Pig's Eye liked a drink now and then, with only short intervals between now and then. He was a drunk. It occurred to him that most men likewise took a drink or two on special occasions, such as weekends or weekdays, and so he decided to go into business of importing, manufacturing, and selling booze.

The best place to set up a grog shop on a remote frontier? Why, near a military post of course, soldiers being a notoriously thirsty lot. Fort St. Anthony (later renamed Fort Snelling) had been built at the confluence of the Minnesota and Mississippi Rivers. The men stationed there were bored and not a little resentful that their commandant had decided to make them plant, harvest, and grind their own wheat because of the difficulty in obtaining supplies on the frontier. For the soldiers, it was bad enough being stationed on the edge of nowhere; now they were expected to become farmers too. They were ready to enjoy a drink off base. Pig's Eye set up his bar in a dugout cave on the riverbank across the Mississippi River from the fort. Pig's Eye sold large quantities of a cheap, potent whiskey known as Red Eye, named for the morning-after appearance of those who had imbibed enthusiastically. Pig's Eye claimed that his whiskey was especially good, having been aged for several entire weeks. His patrons claimed that, when Pig's Eye's blind eye looked the same as his other eye, it was time to stumble home.

Pig's Eye did not discriminate in vending his liquor. He served soldiers, traders, Indians, pioneers, and boatmen alike and quickly was doing a great business. His reputation spread quickly throughout the territory and boat captains began heading for "Pig's Eye's Landing" instead of Mendota. The entire community that was growing around his bar was becoming known as Pig's Eye. The man himself was forced to abandon his saloon and leave town when he couldn't pay back a ninety-dollar mortgage on his little property. Maybe his prices were just too low, or maybe the large quantities of his own Red Eye that he consumed had clouded his business judgment. He died on the banks of Lake Superior, a victim, it is said, of "a disease resulting from his own vices."

The spirit of Pig's Eye, complete with his bad eye, still likes to hang out in saloons near the waterfront in the city he founded by accident and luck. Just don't look for Pig's Eye on the map. It is now known as St. Paul.

Old Bets Is Still at It

According to some, Old Bets is still around, at least as a spirit. Old Bets was a Sioux; her birth name was Azryamankawan, which might explain why whites preferred to use Old Bets, which was shortened from Betsy, which was shortened from Elizabeth, the name she took when she became a Christian. The "old" part was encouraged by Bets herself, who gloried in her advanced age as further evidence of her supernatural wisdom and psychic powers. For the final two decades of her life, she'd been assuring gullible clients that she was a century old. When she died on May 1, 1873, her family estimated her age at about eighty-five, as no birth certificates were issued for Sioux on the frontier in the 1780s.

Old Bets made a living of sorts by predicting the future for folks, and was a well-known character in old St. Paul. Not that the world is short of fortune tellers, but Old Bets earned particular fame thanks to two startling facts: Her predictions were completely true and her own death did not end her career.

A tragedy in her youth had confirmed Old Bets's psychic powers. She had fallen in love with a handsome man, a good hunter and a brave warrior. Somehow, her lover had incurred the displeasure of Bets's older brother, a powerful medicine man and prophet. He forbade the marriage. When Bets touched her brother's hand, she had a terrifying vision of the future. She saw herself covered in the blood of her sweetheart. Bets begged her brother to forgive the unknown transgressions of her intended but to no avail. The young lovers decided to run away together into the forest and live as man and wife. Bets's brother tracked them down and struck down the new husband, just as she had foreseen.

Bets, carried home by her violent brother, eventually married and bore several children. Her visions of the future continued, rather to her distress. Bets was peaceful enough by nature but she was not a pacifist. Once, when her people were subjected to an unprovoked attack by rival Chippewa, the struggle left ten Chippewa warriors wounded on the field of battle. Bets took an ax and pounded in their skulls one at a time. Why? "Because I could see a future in which they recovered from their wounds and attacked my family," Bets said.

In the infamous "Sioux Outbreak" of 1862, Bets sided with the whites and warned many isolated settlers on the frontier to flee to safety. She had had visions of a full-scale war wiping out her people and tried to prevent that. Many in her own family were killed.

Without family, without land, without any assets other than her visions of the future, Old Bets took to begging on the streets of St. Paul. Her pride insisted that she give something in return, so Old Bets started trading her visions for food. Her preferred style was to ask passersby to buy her a meal, which she would share with her benefactor. After a sociable meal, Old Bets would clasp her benefactor's hands in hers and stare into their eyes, then tell them of their future. She loved to tell about future good news but also reported future problems and disasters. Foreknowledge was a very mixed blessing, she would say. If Old Bets took your hands in hers, you had to be prepared to hear predictions of sorrow as well as of joy. Old Bets always was honest and direct, which caused some to avoid her company. Nonetheless, she was a beloved character. The local Chamber of Commerce supported her during her final illness and paid for her funeral.

It is said that her ghost occasionally strolls the streets of St. Paul, looking for a lunch partner. Are you brave enough to learn about your future? It will just cost you a meal and perhaps a few nights' sleep. Knowing the future isn't always a good thing.

The Alluring Ghost

This particular ghost is said to haunt the vicinity of Seventh and Marquette in downtown Minneapolis. This phantom is quite selective in its materializations, appearing only to solitary, handsome men of prosperous appearance. The more evidence of prosperity apparent on the man, the more dazzling the smile he earns from this spirit. The phantom is that of a beautiful young woman. She appears in the essence of late-Victorian high fashion, wearing a long dress of silk trimmed in lace and colorful bows. Her whole figure is that perfect image of full ripeness much favored in the late nineteenth century. Her flashing eyes and beguiling smile indicate that wondrous pleasures are available—at a price.

As the observer watches in increasingly horrified fascination, the spirit of this youthful beauty ages rapidly before his eyes. The flawless, creamy skin sags and wrinkles. Dark pouches develop under the fading blue of her eyes. Her vibrant red hair becomes streaked with gray. The watcher's delight is rapidly replaced by revulsion, tinged with pity. The gorgeous young woman has become a pitiful, ill-kempt hag, all in a matter of seconds. Then, suddenly, the disturbing image is gone, dissolving in a swirl of dust.

The ghost is thought to be that of Anna Robinson, a scullery maid from Minneapolis who once sat on the throne of a queen. She went from making beds in a cheap boardinghouse to gracing the beds of the rich and famous.

Anna was born in poverty and she died in poverty, but in the sweet, fleeting days of her youthful beauty, she lived a fantasy life of glamour and splendor. She parlayed her natural assets of physical beauty, wit and, shall we say, flexible ethics into a career as a courtesan—a very high-priced prostitute.

Anna's mother, a poor widow with three children to feed, ran a boardinghouse catering to theatrical folks. Anna cleaned rooms, served meals, and washed dishes. As she blossomed into a lovely young lady, she was sent to theaters to solicit business. She was quite good at the soliciting part. Anna's obvious physical charms earned her roles onstage and soon she was a noted actress. While appearing on Broadway, she attracted the attention of a visiting English nobleman, the Earl of Rosslyn. The two were married in 1905.

As the Countess of Rosslyn, Anna was introduced into high society throughout Europe. Soon, she was notorious for ignoring her marriage vows in return for expensive gifts. She dazzled men into presenting her with dazzling jewels. Her most famous conquest was Leopold, King of Belgium. Leopold had amassed a vast personal fortune through ruthless exploitation of what was once the largest private plantation in the world—the African Congo, eighty times the size of Belgium. Bewitched by her charms, Leopold once let Anna sit on the queen's throne—naked and in private. He gave her a fabulous diamond choker that she seldom took off.

As Anna aged, her beauty faded and her admirers faded away too. Her husband divorced her. Poor and friendless, she lost her mind. Unknown, penniless, and insane, she died in New York in 1917. No wonder that her ghost chooses to appear in Minneapolis, where she first realized that her seductive powers could take her into realms of wealth and glory.

The Ghost of Dan Patch

The magnificent stallion races past the spectators, a mahogany streak that never falters. All of those who claim to have seen him agree that the horse's speed was remarkable, especially so because the handsome beast was pacing, not running at a full gallop. A pacing horse, unlike one at full gallop, always has two legs on the ground, alternating between the right and left sides of the animal. Pacers are directed by a driver riding in a tiny sulky behind the horse rather than a jockey astride. Pacing races were very popular a century ago, and one pacer stood out as the superstar of the sport.

Allegedly, the incredibly fast pacer who flashes past the lucky few who've seen him is a ghost: the phantom of Dan Patch.

The best time and place to witness this rare ghost is said to be in the late afternoon in early September at the state fairgrounds in Falcon Heights north of St. Paul. It was there, at five o'clock on September 8, 1906, that Dan Patch set a new world record of 1:55 in pacing a mile. That's forty five feet a second. The record, which stood for more than fifty years, made Dan Patch an international celebrity. And if the witnesses of his ghostly races are to be believed, it also earned him a kind of immortality.

After setting the new record, Dan Patch traveled all around the country in his own railroad car, appearing in exhibition races. He paced the mile in less than two minutes seventy-three times and lowered his own record fourteen times. No other pacer in history has been so fast so consistently. According to his driver, Dan Patch never needed encouragement and never felt a whip. The horse was not nervous or high-strung, rather unusual for a thoroughbred harness horse. He is said to have been highly intelligent.

Few animals become ghosts, although living dogs and cats are famously sensitive to the presence of spirits. The most frequently seen supernatural animals are crows, owls, ravens, and wolves, the notorious harbingers of approaching death. Other than Dan Patch, phantom horses are usually associated with ghostly carriages coming to take the souls of the condemned.

As a colt, Dan Patch was purchased for an unheard-of price of $60,000 by Marion Savage, a Minneapolis businessman. After Dan Patch set the world record, Savage turned down $180,000 for him. The man and the horse developed a strong bond. Wherever Dan Patch went, Marion Savage went with him. Dan Patch died of a heart ailment on July 11, 1916. In what may not have been a coincidence, his owner died the next day.

The Girl in the Dog Suit

The girl in the dog suit—or maybe it really is just a dog—is very happy and playful. Her family, even those who are skeptical about reincarnation, is grateful for the continual morale boost of that little creature's presence in their home.

Is it possible that the spirit of a deceased person could return to earth in the form of another living creature? That is a pretty weighty question, and one that a St. Paul family whom we'll call the Jacksons has had to face. Their story begins with a prolonged tragedy and ends with a note of hope and acceptance that life goes on, in one sense or another.

Losing a child is one of the worst emotional traumas anyone can experience. The Jacksons knew, for many sad months, that the shadow of death was hovering over their beloved daughter, Sofia. Shortly after having been diagnosed with her fatal illness, Sofia had described a delightful fantasy to her parents. She had decided that she would avoid the responsibilities and challenges of adulthood by wearing a dog suit. Grownups, she observed, had to go off to work, grumbling about the inconvenient necessity of earning a living. Dogs, on the other hand, had it easy. As Sofia saw it, dogs simply provided love, loyalty, and laughs to their human families and, in return, all the dog's wants were met. "So, I'll make myself a dog suit out of fur and pretend I'm a dog and live happily ever after," Sofia stated.

Was this just a charming fantasy or was it a six-year old's poetic perception of reincarnation? Would Sofia's spirit return to them in the form of a dog?

About three months after Sofia's funeral, a bouncy little puppy showed up at the family's front door. It was a King Charles spaniel, a breed renowned for its affectionate good nature. The dog barked, the door was opened, the dog slipped in, and the family had a furry new member. How could they resist such enthusiastic love lavished on them by such a precious little pup? She had no collar and no one responded to the "found" notice the Jacksons placed in local newspapers. The veterinarian pronounced the puppy to be in excellent health and complimented the Jacksons on their good fortune.

The newest family member, as the Jacksons thought of her, soon was wearing a handsome collar with her name, Joy, inscribed upon it. Joy certainly was appropriate to the dog's personality and, incidentally, was Sofia's middle name. Sofia comes from the Greek for "wisdom," and certainly, if the Jacksons' late daughter's spirit has managed to return in a "dog suit" as she fantasized, she chose wisely in taking the form of a joy-giving little dog. And if Joy is just a dog after all, she, in her way, is consoling her human family with the thought that life does go on, figuratively if not literally.

The Shade of the Empire Builder

The image appears and disappears so quickly that the observers doubt their own eyesight. If the image is real, though, there is no confusion about who the witnesses have just seen. After all, they are in James J. Hill's restored mansion at 240 Summit Avenue in St. Paul, and the many portraits of James Hill himself certainly match the fleeting phantom they glimpsed.

The ghost, typically seen in the library of the fabulous house, takes the form of a bald man with a high, domed forehead and a bushy beard and mustache. In the few seconds in which the phantom is visible, he seems to be quite agitated. His eyes flash with the determination and driving ambition that characterized the man in life. Meet the shade of the Empire Builder, a nickname in which James Jerome Hill took justifiable pride.

In another time and in a different place, James J. Hill might well have founded a political empire rather than the economic empire he built in the Pacific Northwest. His visionary zeal and organizational talents could have marshaled vast armies and seized thrones.

Hill, born in Ontario, Canada, arrived in St. Paul at the age of eighteen. He took a job keeping the books for a steamboat company and also acted as a shipping agent for railroads and Canadian fur exporters. He came to fully appreciate the key role transportation systems played in economic development. He soon purchased the steamboat company he worked for, and turned a small local railroad into the Great Northern Railway. This rail line stretched 1,800 miles from St. Paul to Seattle. James Hill foresaw that, someday, trans-Pacific trade would rival trans-Atlantic trade. He founded a steamship line to link Seattle with Japan, China, and Korea. In order to protect his interests, he also bought up the Northern Pacific Railroad, the Great Northern's chief competitor.

James was not the typical ruthless and selfish robber baron of his day. He understood that the prosperity of his railroads was linked to the prosperity and productivity of the regions the rails served. In order to lure farmers to the once-desolate northern plains, he cut fares for immigrants to a maximum of ten dollars to any place on his rail lines. Would-be settlers could rent a whole boxcar for ten dollars and fill it with building materials, tools, household goods, farm implements, and seed. This farsighted generosity paid great dividends later on, when Hill's rail lines paralleled the prosperous farms and towns.

Hill was also generous to churches and charities. Although not a Catholic, for example, he donated fifty thousand dollars towards building the Cathedral of St. Paul.

Why is Hill's ghost, as revealed to visitors to his restored house, seemingly tense and concerned? Psychics believe that a person's most intense and focused mental and emotional experiences can leave psychic imprints in the rooms or areas in which they occurred. James Hill's greatest business challenge was his struggle to retain control over the Northern Pacific Railroad.

It was in April of 1901 that Hill's ownership of the Northern Pacific was challenged. Edward Harriman of New York had control of the Union Pacific Railroad, Hill's chief competitor for transcontinental traffic. Both companies needed to buy the Burlington Railroad in order to control a route to Chicago, where they could link with eastern railroads. After an expensive competition, Hill bought the Burlington. Harriman then decided to challenge Hill for control of the Northern Pacific. On April 25, stock in the Northern Pacific was selling at $107 a share. Harriman and Hill both began buying stock at any price. By May 9, the stock was $1,000 a share and the stock market was in turmoil. A sudden price collapse could have caused a financial panic. With his empire teetering on the brink, Hill sought a truce with Harriman and allowed Union Pacific trains to travel on the Burlington's tracks to Chicago. The "Great Railroad War" of 1901 was over. Hill kept his railroads, and all his money.

His ghost may still be reliving those tense days when his wealth hung in the balance. It would explain why his phantom is so engrossed that it never seems to notice the living souls who now tour his impressive home. It wouldn't be polite to distract the spirit of the Empire Builder.

The Untrustworthy Ghost

The man's appearance doesn't inspire trust. He looks as though he went to a costume party a week ago and hasn't changed clothing or bathed since. His once-white shirt is stained and wrinkled. His eighteenth-century-style trousers and greatcoat are worn and dusty. Once he speaks, though, it is clear that he is a charmingly persuasive man and a capable salesman. He is also a ghost. When his practiced sales pitch fails to impress, his image simply fades away, leaving the target of his attention wondering if he or she just imagined the whole thing.

What the man was attempting to sell on the streets of St. Paul certainly grabs one's interest, at least until the sheer implausibility of it brings one back to reality. He is selling land, lots of it, and at an attractive price. The man is offering, in whole or in subdivided parts, 200,000 square miles of land in Minnesota and Wisconsin. Only cash is accepted. He happily shows his original land grant, a gift to him from the Sioux Indians. The document is dated April 1767. It purports to transfer to one Jonathan Carver a tract of land running down the east bank of the Mississippi River from St. Anthony's Falls to Lake Pepin where the Chippewa River joins the Mississippi. From that point, the claim runs due east for five days' travel (a day's travel to equal twenty English miles), then due north for six days' travel, and then takes a straight line back to St. Anthony's Falls. This area would include the present Minneapolis campus of the state university, most of St. Paul, numerous cities and towns in Wisconsin, and some of the nation's best farmland.

Jonathan Carver was an early explorer of the upper Minnesota territories during the 1760s. Born in England, he claimed to be a fearless explorer and friend to Native Americans. In April of 1767, he attended the grand council of Sioux chiefs held at a cave in the riverbank where the city of St. Paul would grow up. The Sioux were so happy with Carver that they gave him all that land, or so he said. The Sioux were to retain fishing rights on all water bodies, and hunting rights on all lands not fenced and cultivated. The Sioux later sold chunks of that same land to the U.S. government in exchange for sixty gallons of whiskey, which must have produced a memorable party.

Jonathan went back to England and wrote a bestselling book about his adventures. He married and started a family, perhaps forgetting that he already had a wife and children living in Connecticut. When he died, he left his whole Sioux land grant to his English wife. He also left his entire land grant to his American wife. His English wife sold the land to a man who was murdered on his way to Minnesota, never to appear on "his" land. The heirs of Carver's American wife sold all his Sioux lands to Edward Houghton, a Vermont gentleman, in 1794. They then sold the same claim to a Reverend Peters in 1806.

Peters and Houghton fought out ownership of the land in the courts until 1823. Then, a Congressional committee decreed that the Sioux never had a valid claim to any lands east of the Mississippi. The land was not theirs to give away or sell (twice). The land was not Jonathan Carver's to give to his wives, nor was it the legal property of his American relatives, who sold it twice. It's not yours either, so put away your dreams of wealth. Carver's ghost is as untrustworthy as the living man.

Welcoming Committee

It had been a physically exhausting and emotionally draining day. Not that it took much these days to wear Alice out. She was eighty-four years old, after all. Even a considerably younger person would find that moving day demanded all their energy and then some. It was, Alice reflected, only her third move in her entire life, and it was not as joyous an event as the first two. She understood, even agreed with, her son's reasoning that living by herself in a four-bedroom suburban house set on a large lot no longer made any sense. St. Paul had a wide variety of good assisted living facilities and she now was a "guest" in one.

After a prolonged goodbye with her family, Alice at last was alone in her new home—her final home, most likely. She must have drifted off in her lounge chair, awakening abruptly to see two unfamiliar elderly ladies sitting comfortably on her old velvet sofa. "Oh, dear," said one. "We've startled you. We didn't mean to." They explained that they were the welcoming committee—not the official welcoming group with their forced smiles and unwelcome assumption that Alice would join several social groups—but the "real" welcome committee of volunteers whose experiences there could provide sound, unbiased advice.

Now, Alice had a real talent for detecting, as she put it in polite company, "male bovine excrement." Her B.S. meter had been fine-tuned by forty years as a fourth-grade teacher, dealing with wily students, unrealistic parents, and devious administrators. The unofficial welcomers were, she decided, the real thing. The women's blunt, concise assessments of the staff and other "guests" proved to be always spot-on.

It was a little disconcerting to Alice to realize that she never saw her welcomers outside her own apartment. Eleanor and Ginny, as they introduced themselves, never appeared in the dining room, TV lounge, game room, or library. And they never knocked. Alice would look up from her book or awaken from a catnap, and there they'd be. More puzzling was Eleanor and Ginny's infallible knowledge of the future. "You might want to apply for Mrs. Hanson's room," advised Eleanor. "It faces the garden and gets less street noise." "But she's in good shape and only seventy-two," replied Alice. Eleanor just gave her a sad smile and said, "She'll have a fatal stroke in two weeks." Within three weeks Alice was enjoying her new garden view.

Then there was the case of Beverly, the pushy social director who wouldn't take no for an answer when urging Alice to join the bridge club. "Don't fret it," advised Ginny, "She won't be here much longer. She's due for a fatal car accident next Friday." That too came to pass. "How do you know these things?" asked Alice when the committee visited next. "We thought you'd already guessed," replied Ginny. "We are spirits ourselves. And our main purpose is to welcome you to the spirit world when the time comes."

Bibliography

Books

American Automobile Association. *North Central*. Heathrow, FL: AAA Publishing, 2010.

Beckley, Timothy. *The UFO Silencers*. New Brunswick, NJ: Inner Light, 1990.

Blegen, Theodore. *Minnesota: A History of the State*. Minneapolis: University of Minnesota Press, 1963.

Botkin, B. A., ed. *A Treasury of American Folklore*. New York: Crown Publishers, 1944.

Carpenter, Allan, and Carl Provorse. *The World Almanac of the USA*. Mahwah, NJ: World Almanac Books, 1996.

Clark, Jerome. *Unexplained!* Canton, MI: Visible Ink Press, 1999.

Coleman, Loren. *Mysterious America*. London: Faber and Faber, 1983.

Daegling, David. *Bigfoot Exposed*. Walnut's Creek, CA: Altamira Press, 2004.

Dorson, Richard. *American Folklore*. Chicago: University of Chicago Press, 1959.

Epting, Chris. *The Birthplace Book: A Guide to Birth Sites of Famous People, Places and Things*. Mechanicsburg, PA: Stackpole Books, 2009.

Explore Minnesota Tourism Office. *Explore Minnesota: 2011 Travel Guide*. St. Paul: State of Minnesota, 2011.

Federal Writers' Project of the Works Progress Administration. *The Minnesota Arrowhead Country*. Chicago: Albert Whitman, 1941.

Federal Writers' Project of the Works Progress Administration. *The WPA Guide to Minnesota*. St. Paul: Minnesota Historical Society Press, 1985. First published 1938 by Viking.

Green, John. *Encounters with Bigfoot*. Surrey, BC: Hancock House, 1994.

Guiley, Rosemary. *The Encyclopedia of Ghosts and Spirits*. New York: Facts on File, 1992.

Harper, Charles. *Haunted Houses: Tales of the Supernatural*. Philadelphia: J. B. Lippincott, 1930.

Hauck, Dennis. *Haunted Places: The National Directory*. New York: Penguin-Putnam, 2002.

Krantz, Grover. *Bigfoot/Sasquatch Evidence*. Surrey, BC: Hancock House, 1999.

Krantz, Les. *America by the Numbers: Facts and Figures from the Weighty to the Way-Out*. Boston: Houghton Mifflin, 1993.

Lass, William. *Minnesota: A Bicentennial History*. New York: Norton, 1977.

Myers, Arthur. *A Ghost Hunter's Guide to Haunted Landmarks, Parks, Churches and Other Public Places*. Chicago: Contemporary Books, 1993.

———. *The Ghostly Register*. New York: McGraw-Hill / Contemporary Books, 1986.

Norman, Michael, and Beth Scott. *Historic Haunted America*. New York: Tor, 1995.

Pickering, David. *Casell Dictionary of Superstitions*. London: Casell, 1995.

Potter, Merle. *101 Best Stories of Minnesota*. Minneapolis: Harrison and Smith, 1931.

Skinner, Charles. *American Myths and Legends*. Detroit: Gale Research Co., 1974.

Stein, George, ed. *The Encyclopedia of the Paranormal*. Buffalo: Prometheus, 1996.

Taylor, Troy. *The Haunting of America: Ghosts and Legends from America's Past*. Alton, IL: Whitechapel Productions, 2001.

Thompson, C. J. S. *The Mystery and Lore of Apparitions*. London: Harold Shaylor, 1930.

Online Sources

"Famous Ghosts, Page 2." *Legends of America*. LegendsofAmerica.com/GH-celebrityghosts2.html.

Ghost Eyes. GhostEyes.com.

"Haunted Places in Minnesota." *The Shadowlands*. TheShadowLands.net/places/Minnesota.html

"Heroes and Champions." *American Folklore*. AmericanFolklore.net/ff.html.

Acknowledgments

THIS IS MY TWELFTH BOOK PUBLISHED BY STACKPOLE BOOKS AND WRITten under the friendly guidance and skillful expertise of my editor, Kyle Weaver. Associate editor Brett Keener again piloted the manuscript through the production process with his meticulous attention to detail. My sincere thanks to both of them and to the rest of Stackpole's expert staff.

Elizabeth Eckardt once again transformed my untidy handwritten manuscript into a polished product. She is a paragon of efficiency and patience. Steve Eckardt kept my laptop computer healthy and obedient; he is a natural teacher. Herb Richardson, an old friend and colleague, tracked down some books I needed. The friendly and knowledgeable professional librarians at McGowan Library in Pitman, New Jersey, and at Rowan University's Campbell Library provided timely assistance.

I wish to thank the enthusiastically helpful staffs of the Explore Minnesota Tourism office, the Minnesota Department of Natural Resources, and the Minnesota Historical Society.

As always, my dear wife, Diane, patiently tolerated the semiorganized clutter of books, notes, and maps that accompanies a book project. No author ever had a more loving and supportive partner. Thanks again, my sweetheart.

About the Author

CHARLES A. STANSFIELD JR. TAUGHT GEOGRAPHY AT ROWAN UNIVERSITY in Glassboro, New Jersey, for forty-one years and published fifteen textbooks on cultural and regional geography. In the course of his research, he realized that stories of ghosts and other strange phenomena reflect the history, culture, economy, and even physical geography of a region, leading him to collect tales from all parts of the country. He is the author of *Haunted Presidents* and ten other titles in the Stackpole Books Haunted Series: *Haunted Colorado, Haunted Washington, Haunted Arizona, Haunted Northern California, Haunted Southern California, Haunted Ohio, Haunted Vermont, Haunted Maine, Haunted Jersey Shore*, and *Haunted New Jersey*.

Other Titles in the
Haunted Series